Lesia Cartelli is a courageous soul who has met and learned from the incredible hardship life has given her. Her reward is a bounty of help to offer others as they move through their own pain. Our reward is her enormous heart and commitment to guide us through.

—MARK NEPO,
author of *New York Times* best seller,
The Book of Awakening and
Seven Thousand Ways to Listen

When powerful stories, deep insight, and an extraordinary communication style come together, magic happens. I will tell you from experience—Lesia Cartelli makes magic happen when she speaks. She is able to share profound truths that resonate for everyone in her audience. It is a special gift. You cannot help but fall in love with Lesia, but intriguingly, when you hear her speak, you also end up loving yourself and feeling more capable of mastering whatever demands the world has of you.

—SUSAN N. FOWLER, Senior Consulting Partner
The Ken Blanchard Companies

Lesia Stockall Cartelli

Heart of Fire

An Intimate Journey of Pain, Love, and Healing

"Lesia Cartelli is a courageous soul who has met and learned from the incredible hardship life has given her. Our reward is her enormous heart and commitment to guide us through."

—MARK NEPO, *New York Times* best-selling author of *The Book of Awakening*

Heart of Fire
Lesia Stockall Cartelli

For bulk sales contact the publisher or author at:
Carlyle Press, 4405 Manchester Ave, Suite 101, Encinitas, CA 92024

Cover and Interior Design: Rebecca Finkel, F+P Graphic Design
Publisher: Carlyle Press
Publishing Consultant: Judith Briles, The Book Shepherd
Editor: John Maling, Editing By John

Library of Congress Catalog Number:
ISBN soft cover: 978-0-9904307-3-5
eISBN: 978-0-9904307-0-4
Audio book: 978-0-990430702-0-8

Categories for cataloging and shelving:
1. Inspiration   2. Trauma   3. Health   4. Success

Printed in the USA

Prologue

We all have a birthday. We celebrate with family, and friends—or even alone.

This book is about the birthday we experience that calls for no celebration but where fear, trauma and love come crashing onto the same path deep inside our hearts. And with courage and passion we choose to create a new. Then we feast on searching for the next awakening, like nectar sequestering our thirst. It's always in front of us. Only if we choose to see it.

The natural gas explosion was my first "birthday" of awakening.

Your "spiritual birthday" might be marked by the death of a loved one, a birth of a child, a traumatic accident, or any turning point in your path where your life becomes dramatically different, where you handle the situation in a decidedly new way. You might think of these as deep contracts you've made with your soul, sometimes on a level you can't see, but you feel.

Our spiritual birthdays come in many forms, often camouflaged as a challenge.

Reading this book perhaps you'll see how our challenges and unique coincidences are the training grounds for what happens next in our lives. My hope is that my story will help you look at your challenges and struggles as your greatest teachers and clear blessings for what comes on your path.

This is my story. Some people may wonder why certain details were left out. Why others were included. This was my decision. Some things in life are sacred and must rest in my heart, forever. Others may wonder how I ever found courage to speak from my open heart. It's my truth. This book is from me, and how some of you have played an immeasurable part in my life, both superior and difficult.

Some of the names have been altered to protect what is hallowed. Honoring our boundaries.

I'm sharing my journey in the hopes that you look at your own path and acknowledge all situations as a true gift.

I hope my story will leave your eyes open to tomorrow, your heart full with grace and love, enough to last you a lifetime.

To Bruce,

my rock.

Acknowledgments

It is with heartfelt honor I acknowledge the people in my life who have held my hand in encouragement and comfort.

I'm grateful for my devoted husband, who often asked, "Are you finished writing yet?"

My heart is busting with gratitude for Diane and our early morning coastal walks. Having her cradle my words of how difficult it is to write about deep painful situations followed by shared laughter from stepping on dog poo at daybreak, she's the kind of friend we all covet.

To my editor, Tershia, when she'd call me, rather than communicate through email, I knew I had to dig deeper inside of me. She was my pusher, forever holding up a mirror, encouraging me to write about situations I tried to gloss over. The painful stuff no one wants to relive.

To my tribe of women who became my corner pillars, holding up what is sacred, brushing me off when I fell and pushing me forward when I was stuck.

I'm deeply grateful to Judith, my book shepherd, who flew into my path, updated my wings and led me where I needed to go.

To my girls who had the courage to come to angel faces. When one asks me if I have children, I touch my heart and reply, "I have heart children, hundreds of them."

To my family who always made me laugh and who feared what would end up in this book.

To all the professionals in the burn and trauma world who God placed in my path, I will always feel gratitude in my heart when I think of you.

To those who believed in me, more than I believed in myself and encouraged me to share my story, I thank you.

Contents

CHAPTER ONE
Circus Life......................... 1

CHAPTER TWO
Explosion.......................... 21

CHAPTER THREE
Sinking 39

CHAPTER FOUR
Pushed Into Purpose.......... 63

CHAPTER FIVE
Burn Camp....................... 87

CHAPTER SIX
Back Into the Fire............ 111

CHAPTER SEVEN
Blind Dreams.................. 133

CHAPTER EIGHT
Angel Faces Delivered 157

CHAPTER NINE
Risks and Rewards 173

CHAPTER TEN
Healing Hearts 187

CHAPTER ELEVEN
Watching Courage............ 205

CHAPTER TWELVE
Bouquet of Many Layers ... 223

Afterword...................... 227

About the Author............. 233

CHAPTER ONE

Circus Life

*Trusting in yourself is
sometimes all the trust we'll ever know.*

No infant knows what family and circumstances are on the other end of the birth canal, but whatever a newborn's conditions are, they soon feel routine. And, I believe, they are our soul's preparation for the journey to come. I arrived, one Sunday in late May, into a loving family of surprises, disruption, and invention. As unpredictable as my childhood was, the horrendous calamity to come was nowhere in sight.

When my parents met as teenagers while ice-skating in Detroit, "slippery" became a metaphor for their life together.

My mother Gloria was young and stunningly gorgeous. She was the oldest of a large poor Polish family. My father

Don, equally as handsome, was an only child. His father was from Nova Scotia and his mother from deep in the Black Hills of Arkansas. My father scooped Gloria up off the ice as she scrambled from a fall. Entranced by the rescue, they fell in love and were soon married in Detroit, Michigan. Pregnancy was never far away from women in the 1950s. By the time my parents were 25-years-old, all five of us had been born, making our family's security that much more slippery. Everyone in the family seemed to cultivate his or her own approach to navigating the uncertainty each day delivered. I am the youngest so my focus was keeping up with the others while keeping the drama from swallowing me—a big job for a little girl.

Trusting in yourself is sometimes all the trust we'll ever know.

My father could be a lot of fun when he was around, but his coming and going made it seem as if he didn't want to be with us. His profession was a mystery. On school forms, we were supposed to write "salesman" as his occupation. Yet what Dad sold was anyone's guess.

Anything big, gilded or extravagant was apt to appear in our lives. Tugboats, ornate antiques, and ponderous paintings would arrive only to vanish soon after. He would return with furs and luxury cars when what we really needed was money to pay the utilities. Like a lot of women of the time, my mother was a stay-at-home mom. However, comparing her circumstances to other mothers, I'd say she had a special challenge caring for us amidst the chaos my impetuous father attracted.

With my brothers and sisters, I spent most weekend nights peeking through the banister watching our parents and their friends partying. Their declining behavior was its own lesson on the dangers of drinking too much alcohol. Sure, we kids got caught peeking through the stairs and sent back to bed, though as soon as we'd hear the boom of Chubby Checker's "C'mon baby, let's do the twist," we'd be up and cavorting again, making the most of every moment.

We moved most every year, sometimes more often than that and always in a big hurry. My first memory of a place we stayed long enough to call "home" was a long white carriage house, belonging on an estate that bordered Lake St. Clair. Our house had black window shutters. The seven garages below each had large round iron turnstiles in the center. These turnstiles were originally used decades before to turn the cars around—before cars had reverse.

The carriage house was all but hidden in an eerie wooded grove in upscale Grosse Pointe, Michigan. Between Lake St. Clair and our carriage house was the creepy brick mansion where "Old Man Orin" lived, and he was our constant temptation. We dared each other, over and over again, to climb up his tall staircase, ring his bell, and then scamper for cover in the woods. He seemed to get a kick from scaring us children. Dressed in a dark suit, cane in hand, he'd appear at the front window. That white-faced specter was plenty of motivation not to pester him. Yet there we were, frequently.

Being the youngest, I was always running behind and more terrified than the others screaming, "Wait for me!"

After tripping and falling down the staircase, I took refuge in my room and waited an entire week before playing with my siblings again—an eon for a four-year-old. When chaos like this surfaced, I already knew I could turn inward, hug myself, and trust that this was all happening for a reason. No noise. No demands. No shouting. No tripping. No being left behind. And best of all, I could make this inner peace bigger and more inviting. I didn't recognize this activity as meditation, but that's what it was.

Most children have their own ways of centering themselves, such as playing with their toys, family pet or burying themselves in social media.

After my scrapes healed, my middle sister Cindy proposed that we three youngest walk to the closest store, S. S. Kresge's, to shop for Easter candy. (My sister Chris and brother Danny were still at school.) We had never been off the grounds without our parents. Everything was too far away to walk, so my mother always drove us. For this reason and many others, Cindy's proposal was daring in the extreme. Even at seven-years-old, Cindy was already a bit like my father—an instigator. Anyway, we loved S. S. Kresge's. Who could resist?

With snow coats and hand-me-down boots, the three of us toddled down our long driveway, through the gates, and across the busy street. Cindy led, Darrin was in the middle, and I took up the rear, always trying to catch up. In a late spring storm, snow fell from the sky. Trudging through neighborhoods of large homes, the journey seemed to take forever. By the time we reached the store, my little limbs were spent. S. S. Kresge's had everything from tooth-brushes to toys to medicines. It even had a soda fountain, but Cindy wouldn't suffer any distractions. She grabbed a cart and told Darrin and me to follow her.

"Don't get lost," my domineering sister cautioned us.

We scoured every aisle, putting everything we wanted in the cart. There was no one to tell us "no" except my bossy sister, yet Cindy said nothing no matter how many choco-late bunnies, Barbie Dolls, Slinkys, and Silly Putty I tossed over the side of the cart. Darrin heaped in his favorites, too. We filled the shopping cart to the brim and then proceeded to checkout just like adult customers. People were staring and smiling at us. No doubt my sister felt very grown up. Darrin trusted her. And me? I just wanted to be included.

As we got closer to the cashier, my sister whispered over her shoulder that she didn't want to stay in the line anymore. "Let's go!" She now shouted.

So off we went. We pushed the cart full of our desired goods straight out the door, and no one stopped us!

Making tracks in the snow, Cindy somehow got the cart across the busy street. Since no one was on our heels, we just kept going back through the same neighborhoods. By the time we reached the gates of our property, Cindy and Darrin made a tactical decision to have me push the cart the final stretch through the snow. With my hands barely reaching the handle, I was enslaved, and all the toys and goodies a four-year-old could want were gleaming at me through the bars. I was spellbound. But after that three mile trip, I was also completely tuckered out. As my eyes focused on our house, that same feeling of turning inward surfaced. *Whew! Safe for now.*

Once inside the gates we saw Mom running toward us, shouting with her arms in the air, "Where have you kids been?" Our usually mild-mannered mother continued shouting across the property, "We have been looking for you!" As she got closer, we saw tears of relief running down her face. She seemed pretty glad to see us. "Wow," I thought, "she really does love us." She was usually so focused on meeting our father's demands that I'd often had the feeling of being unnoticed.

Then Mom noticed the cart. "Where in the heck did you kids go, and where did you get all this stuff?" Feeling a sudden yearning to be unnoticed again, I shrank behind my sister, so she could direct her inquisition at Cindy.

"At the store, Mom. You know, the one you take us to," Cindy answered sheepishly.

"WHO PAID FOR ALL OF THIS!?" my mother demanded in a panicked tone.

"No one," Cindy mumbled.

"What?" It wasn't as if Mom was inexperienced with 'suddenly appearing stuff,' but it was usually my father's doing—not that of her three little "innocent" children.

"You darned kids! I was worried sick about you; I was ready to call the police!" Our poor mother had reached the end of her emotional tether. Still crying, she rolled the shopping cart into one of the garages and closed and locked the door. Then she hastened us indoors. We were in trouble. Serious trouble—she sent us to our rooms. I was glad, really, because my room was my sanctuary. Exhausted, I finally lay on my bed. I wondered how long it would take Mom to soften, as she did when Dad arrived with too much of a good thing, and then turn the cart of goodies over to us. *Thanks, Cindy.*

Not too long after the Kresge's caper, my father came home and announced casually that the bull-dozers were coming in a few days and we had to get out.

My father was sure that he was once a king of another land with a crown and magic wand that could do anything.

For Dad to pick up and go was natural and no big deal. For the rest of us, hasty moves were another matter. My mother was outwardly calm and steady, but this was unhappy news. Our reality was full of upheaval. With a heavy sigh and a tight lip, she began throwing things in boxes.

"Where are we going to live, Mom?" I asked. Half-stuffed boxes under her arm, and rushing by me, she replied, "Quickly, kids, get your toys together. We need to pack, now!"

Packing wasn't really my father's thing. There were too many emotions among us, and he had to focus on getting us a place to live. I watched him bolt from the carriage house, mumbling "I'll be back in a little while," like he always did. He returned late that evening. Overhearing the controlled whispers of my siblings, I picked up the familiar scent of fear. *What would tomorrow bring? Where would we go?* Lying in bed and listening to my inner voice, I knew instinctively that the only thing I could rely on was my own self.

The next day we moved four miles away to a large beautiful four-bedroom English Tudor-style house with a large basement. Perhaps this would be our "real home"? The yard was huge and bordered by a deep dark canal. The way my father had abruptly manifested such a place, when he had no money or profession, seemed like magic. As my family carted boxes and antiques inside, I could see the neighbors watching. We had never had neighbors before, except for Mr. Orin. Suddenly, Mr. Orin didn't seem so bad. I already missed our carriage house.

Were the bulldozers tearing it down today? Why? Was it because we stole stuff just days before?

We stayed more than three years at that house on the canal. That was a long time for our family. The house rested on the down angle of a sharp bridge. Nearly every night joy riders raced over the bridge, we'd hear them all scream and laugh. I actually thought they were laughing at us, at our circus life. I tagged along with my siblings who spent summers inventing games with the neighborhood kids. During snowy winters we retreated to the basement to play hockey with Dad's bent combs and balled up socks. "He shoots and scores!" was a common bellow from my brothers.

The house was full of antique clocks from Denmark, paintings from England, and furniture from Italy. My father was sure that he was once a king of another land. He was fascinated by anything that was castle-like; red velvet, swords, chalices, jewels, and of course, crowns. My dress-up play time often found me in the living room sitting on a royal throne, pretending I was queen, with a fire roaring in the fireplace. I thought it was normal to have a large gold-leafed throne upholstered in crushed red velvet until the sight put neighbor friends agog. This memento is still in my possession, so the queen (that'd be me) can sit and rule.

We watched a small television in a den lined with dark wood and deep red velvet curtains. The room's red leather furniture made it the perfect setting for my after-school ritual of watching *Dark Shadows,* a vampire show.

Amidst my father's chaos, my mother had insisted that we attend Catholic schools. She knew we needed consistency in the home given my father's behavior. She also knew the nuns could give us children a dependable spiritual path. At St. Ambrose Elementary School, I met Jenny Lou who lived on the next street. Every Sunday, we walked to church together, filling my hunger for God. Jenny Lou wore a brace on her leg. Jenny Lou looked different. I felt different but I felt more like myself when I was at church, enjoying the opportunity to pause and reflect on my connection to forces I could feel but not see.

Everyone around us knew my father was eccentric and fun loving. Unfortunately, his dark side surfaced when he drank and he drank often. Frequently, Dad would simply disappear for days. My mother worried and wept yet did her best to hide her angst, while working hard to keep her young tribe on track. When Dad was home, my parents quarreled frequently, usually over money and my father's "extraordinary" ideas.

How is it that children, who are so young, feel responsible for their parents' behavior? The desire to fix other people's problems can last a lifetime. Would you still do anything to fix, smooth over and escape from the pain that lurks behind your childhood walls?

Unexpectedly, my parents opened up a nightclub in Detroit called The Poison Apple. It was a unique saloon with antiques as furnishings, red sawdust covering the floor, a signature drink, and folk entertainment. They hired a midget named Jackie to serve hot fresh popcorn from an antique popcorn machine. On weekend nights, people lined up around the block to get inside.

Weekends were Mom's chance to dress up, get out of the house, and head to "The Apple." Greeting friends and other customers, bartending, waitressing and keeping their staff in order, she enjoyed our nightclub as much as Dad.

As Mom primped for evenings at The Apple, I sat on her bed and watched her fix her beautiful blonde hair. After she pulled on shiny black high-heeled boots and painted on red lipstick, I'd help her zip up her black cocktail dress, and find her gloves to match. She was very classy, a blonde Jackie Onassis type.

She'd order us a pizza, give Cindy money for pop and chips, and then dish orders about "behaving" while my father and she were out. (Chris and Danny were out, too.) The pizza-delivery man had seemed creepy to us, in the past. He had wanted to come in and use our bathroom. We didn't let him, even though it was pouring rain. Without telling our parents what had happened, we talked about how letting him in might have changed our lives forever. We were determined on this particular night to secure our pizza without letting this character scare us again.

"I've got a great idea!" Cindy announced. "Let's pretend we are Mom and Dad. Lesia, you can get on Darrin's shoulders. We'll put one of Mom's blonde wigs and some earrings on you, then pull one of her full-length dresses over you and Darrin." I could see from Darrin's expression that he was not enthusiastic about this.

"I'll wear Dad's suit and slick my hair back," she announced. Having hatched yet another daring scheme, indomitable Cindy was not to be stopped. As the youngest, I was pressed as always by the "you HAVE to do it, 'cause I said so" rationale. Winning through intimidation, family-style.

"No way," Darrin objected. Darrin was beyond shy and the thought of my sitting on his shoulders terrified him. A lot of things terrified Darrin. Darrin never wanted to be in the front of the line on anything, which was unfortunate for him in a family where the three-ring circus was the norm. Not wanting other children to see our mother delivering him in a Ford Model T, black sleek limousine, or eventually conveyances that required horses, Darrin would insist on being dropped off a block before school. It was all too much for him. Now he was to be featured in a flowing cocktail dress?

"You want pizza? Then you're going to do it!" Cindy snarled.

"Yeah, but …" Darrin scrambled to get out of the obligation, but before his words came out, we were already in Mom's closet selecting the perfect outfit. Cindy tossed dresses, wigs, gloves and heels over her shoulders like a seasoned costume designer. My middle sister was a force to reckon with; once she decided on a dress, the plan's trajectory couldn't be reversed.

The tricky part was passing the gold-jeweled gown over my head while I sat on Darrin's shoulders, and still leaving him enough breathable space. He was very unhappy and we didn't want to suffocate him.

"Bend down, Darrin, so I can put the wig and earrings on Lesia," Cindy barked.

I tumbled off his shoulders onto the floor. Thump. "Ouch!" I whimpered.

"C'mon, Darrin," Cindy continued unfazed. "This is serious. Remember that we don't want to get robbed by the pizza man. That's the whole point here."

I had my own apprehensions but I climbed back on a chair, pulling Darrin close enough to hop on his shoulders, again.

"Geez, easy would you, Lesia. Stop moving around!" he squealed.

After much struggle, mission accomplished. Cindy then dressed in my father's dark suit coat. Since she couldn't find pins to make the pants tighter, she elected to hold them up around her waist manually instead. She slicked her hair back, slipped into my father's shoes, and voilà, we were "our parents," ready for anything.

The doorbell rang. On my cue I shouted my best simulation of a mother voice, "Dahling, the pizza man is here!"

"Coming, Gloria," Cindy replied in her new deep voice as she came down the staircase.

Once Cindy was there behind us with her hands busy holding up her pants, I bent to open the door. As the deliveryman thrust the pizza forward, I slipped from Darrin's shoulders. The wig flew off and a dangling earring caught the sleeve of the dress, exposing "Mom's" lower half as the pizza and I toppled head-over-salami onto the now cheesy porch. We were busted.

We tipped the unwitting deliveryman fifty cents, scraped the pizza off the porch, and slammed the door. Another disaster averted, or nearly.

Unlike our performance, The Poison Apple was an overnight success. Famous folk singers like Joni Mitchell, Tim Hazel and *The Three Penny Opera* called our stage their home. We saw big money start to come in. Weekend mornings my mother nestled at our large round dining room table

Pretending to be someone else to hide pain is a skill that can take years to unlearn as we stretch to discover our own beautiful soul. Even so, a learned mask can pull us through tragedy in the meantime. Childhood games that blur boundaries and encourage fantasy can prepare us for coming challenges.

counting bills and coins, while my father was still in bed, hung over. No sooner was he up than the money went right back out again to buy more ornate furniture, artwork, fancy cars, sailing ships, even Chinese Junks.

The hard part was hearing my parents fight when they came home in the wee hours after closing the club. My parents' arguments usually concerned the women at the club who threw themselves at my father, feasting on his charisma, good looks and gift for entertainment. He never pushed them away, it seemed, but rather encouraged it. I heard my mother call him "A player" and older sister Chris would usually take her side.

Occasionally, strange women would show up on our doorstep longing for him. It made me sick. But the truth was that just like everyone else, I was captivated by my father. I felt lucky to learn how to "have fun" and live the high life no matter what was going on. He seemed magical, as though he could do anything. And, of course, he was my dad and would do anything for me.

On my first Catholic communion, my mother went to great lengths to make the occasion a perfect day. She bought me a beautiful white lace dress, knee socks, white shoes and veil. I had it all. After church she invited our relatives down from the farm, and baked brunch including my favorite Jell-O mold. (Remember this was the sixties.) Outside she set up chairs, tables with linens, and decorations for a garden celebration.

My father never went to church with us, and when we returned home for the party, he was not there. Even though I'm sure my mother was tense, everyone was used to his erratic habits so no one made a big deal about him missing his daughter's communion.

Soon after we finished eating, Dad suddenly arrived and he wasn't alone. He was driving a truck full of goats. Yes, goats! He released them into the party. My young friends squealed with delight, while adults scrambled to protect the food.

"Don!" Mom gasped. "Goats, really? What are you doing bringing goats into the city and to our daughter's Holy Communion party!" she shouted.

"Gloria, my daughter can't 'play' with a gold cross for her confirmation," he laughed, "she needs to have fun with goats!"

Such unpredictability made us popular in the neighborhood. The episodes were legend. Among our garages full of antiques was a prized antique fire engine. On Sundays my father would have a cocktail then roll out the fire truck. Every kid within range would jump on and he'd drive us around the streets, sirens blasting.

Being eccentric, my father didn't advertise our nightclub in the local paper. No, instead he bought a hearse—black with large etched glass windows—and parked it in front of the nightclub. On weekends my aunt, an attractive go-go dancer, lay inside the hearse wearing a tiny black bikini—as though she had taken a sip from our signature drink—a "poisoned apple."

One winter Sunday morning, Dad asked Darrin and me, "Hey, kids, want to come with your father for awhile?"

"Sure, where we going?" As we shoved out the door, I saw my mother roll her eyes. This wasn't unusual. When we pulled up to some unknown garages, Dad popped out of the car, and began undoing the numerous large locks. I could hear the whinny of horses. As the large garage door opened, we saw a man holding the reins of two large black stallions, hooked up to the hearse carriage.

Adventure comes with risks, but risks mean we are alive. The results can be good or bad, but the important thing is to continuously reach.

"They're all ready for you, Mr. Stockall." The worker held out the reins to my father.

My father lifted us up onto the carriage seat, then climbed between us and gathered up the reins. Dad handed us ancient style hats. The worker threw wool blankets over our laps and then smacked the horses on their hinds. The horses clicketty-clacked out of the garage into Detroit's wintery streets. The feel of the occasion was surreal. Being a Sunday morning, all shops were closed; roads were empty. Regular folks were at church.

Suddenly police sirens sliced the deafening silence of the falling snow, and their cars rolled up behind us—startling the horses. Fear overcame my brother, who I've already identified as no fan of oddball behavior. As Darrin began to cry, I snuggled closer to my father. When Dad got the horses calmed from the sirens, two Detroit police approached on foot, and I was certain they were going to haul my father off to jail. *What would we do? Could Darrin and I get the carriage and enormous horses back to the garage?*

Now I sank into my fear, keeping my head down and wishing I had stayed home and played in my room, that private sanctuary devoid of horses and policemen.

My father cautiously greeted the stern-looking men in uniform, "Hello, officers."

The tall officer nodded and throwing his gloved hand on the large thin wooded wheel, demanded, "Driver's license and registration please."

As smooth as smooth can be, my father said, "Well, officer, I left my wallet at home. I'm just taking my kids out for a little Sunday ride." The other officer walked around the carriage to my side. I was frozen in fear and not because of the 35-degree weather.

The officer smiled up at me, "You doing all right there, little one?" I nodded sheepishly. My father jumped in, clear but casual, "Officer, she loves horses. It's Sunday and we just wanted to spend a little time together, go for a ride. Everything's good here."

I could feel my brother tighten up under his wool pea coat, and soon another siren was audible. A squad car pulled up. Oh no, I thought, more trouble. Darrin gripped Dad's leg, terrified we were all going to jail. I thought we were all going to jail, too. I started to weep.

You could tell that the officer who had just arrived was more important, clearly the lieutenant. As he strutted over to us, I could hear the relief in my father's voice. "Tim! How the hell are you, man?"

"Hey there, Don. Great entertainment last night at the club. Shirley and I really enjoyed ourselves." The officer seemed oblivious of the horses, carriage, hearse and the two of us weeping on the cold bench. "Say, do you have the woman who drank the poison apple in there? Bit nippy this morning for the lightly clad."

The niceties continued for a few minutes, exchanging memories of good food, swinging music, and the fun bustling crowd.

"Hell, Don, we waited one hour in the snow to get in the door," the lieutenant threw out. Here was the window of opportunity my father sought to escape out of this mess.

"One hour? Well, I won't let that happen again. Tell you what …" he reached in his pocket and pulled out a wooden nickel, signed the back, and handed it to the lieutenant. My father didn't bring his wallet, but he brought wooden nickels?

"The next time you come to The Poison Apple, go straight to my doorman Mike. Present this wooden nickel and you will never need to wait again, promise you." My dad slipped a look to me. We were going to be OK.

The lieutenant turned to the officers, "That will be all, gentleman." With that the officers shook their heads and walked back to their squad car.

My father tipped his hat, wrapped the blanket around us tighter and the horses clicked down the street.

"You kids OK?" he asked us.

"Yeah, Dad, we're OK," my brother whispered. To me that nickel represented freedom. A get-out-of-jail-free card, just like in monopoly. Nonetheless, I wanted to dash to my room and never venture out again.

"Beautiful Sunday morning," Dad murmured, ignoring what we just had been through. "I wonder what the boring people are doing today?"

Sundays were "family day." They might start off nice, often involving an amusement park, a day boating on the lake in a Chinese junk or riding in an antique fire engine. "Rides for everyone," Dad would shout.

One Sunday we were loading our boat, a beautiful Chris-craft Lyman, with provisions to head out for the day. Danny, the family klutz, slipped while carrying a case of libations. He fell backwards on the stairs leading below deck and sliced his head open. There was blood everywhere. I was terrified. Mom and Chris rushed him to the emergency room. After Danny got 25 stitches in his head, Dad insisted on a day of fun anyway, even though Danny lay below deck with his head wrapped in bandages.

Any outing involving Dad could be fun or hair-raising or both. He was a madcap father. Even on the best of days, by dusk or sooner my father's alcohol consumption inevitably brought out his anger and embarrassed us. My mother would plead with him that we needed to go home. Chris would agree.

"Don, the kids have homework," she'd beg, "tomorrow is a school day …" My father often ignored her, or worse, berated her and told her she was "no fun." We would cling to my mother for safety. I hated those Sundays. Our only reprieves were those Sundays when we went to our grandparents for dinner. Promising a safe, loving outcome, those were my favorite Sundays.

Grandpa and Grandma were stable and consistent with their love. Hard to believe they were my father's parents. They lived in the same house for forty years. Grandpa worked at Chrysler's manufacturing plant Monday through Friday, leaving at 5:45 a.m. returning at 3 p.m.

He painted the garage every summer while listening to baseball games on his transistor radio. He kept his car immaculate and maintained, ate liverwurst on Wednesdays, fish on Fridays, grocery shopped every Saturday at Pete and Frank's, and attended church on Sunday. He was the exact opposite of his son.

CHAPTER TWO

Explosion

Grandma, I smell gas.

My grandma was a beautiful southern woman who always wore a fresh flower in her hair, loved to cook, bake pies and banana bread, and had an endless appetite for lavishing love upon us. She would bake all week, scrub floors, clean windows, and tend to their abundant garden, all in preparation for our family Sunday dinner.

At my home, we had a different car every week, with two to four cars parked in the drive, and one license plate so a screwdriver was always handy to change the plate from car to car. My father was as predictable as a slot machine.

In many ways my grandparents held our family together and embraced my mother as their own daughter. They never understood my father's adventurous behavior, but deeply loved him and thought he walked on water, as we all did. Going to my grandparents' home was heaven to me.

One snowy Sunday afternoon, my sister Chris, her boyfriend Paul and I arrived at our grandparents' home. We were expecting Grandma to reach for us with a big southern hug when the door opened. Instead an awful odor assaulted us.

"Eww, what's that smell?" I cringed.

"Grandma, I smell gas!" My sister's voice grew urgent as she rushed to open windows.

"Yes, honey, I know," my grandma blurted in her heavy Arkansas accent. "The gas company came out earlier. The serviceman smelled it too, but he can't come back until tomorrow when he has a full work crew." She helped my sister get fresh air circulating. Soon our cousins arrived.

My grandma kept the small house immaculate. With everyone there though, relatives spilled out in every direction. The house buzzed with chatter and laughter, our happy family. You know how, after an accident, people always describe the moments before something went wrong as seeming so calm, so normal. *That afternoon was not normal—* not at all. The noise seemed to drown in the odor of natural gas mixed with grandma's roast in the oven. I felt sick to my stomach, but the uneasiness was more than physical. A looming anxiety gnawed at me.

Everyone urged my younger cousin Kimmy and me to play downstairs until dinner was ready. I was relieved. Maybe the gas smell wouldn't be as strong down there. As we scampered down the stairs, we decided to play hide 'n seek.

The finished basement was its own warren of niches and blind corners, perfect for the game. I leaned against a metal pipe next to the furnace while counting backwards, "10, 9, 8 ..." Being nine-years-old, I peeked to see where Kimmy would hide. Through barely-open eyes I watched her climb into the storage room under the staircase, a decision that may have saved Kimmy.

Meanwhile, natural gas fumes wafted freely through the house, blown around by the open windows. Just steps from where I counted was a "point of ignition," the furnace's pilot light where a flickering purple-tipped flame waited. That flame changed my life forever.

As I reached the count of three, gas found its mark and detonated a massive explosion. My only safe haven, my grand-parents' house, exploded and I was literally at "ground zero." Colossal balls of fire engulfed everything in a roaring blaze, including me.

The enormous fire storm, wild and devilish, spread with deafening noise. At its epicenter I heard only the roar of the flames, Kimmy screaming, my family screaming, and my own screams. Then abruptly the whole house was flattened.

I was on fire. I needed to get out! Desperate to find an escape, I frantically groped for handholds. Kimmy still screamed from underneath the staircase.

"Get me out of here! Help me ... it's hot in here, I'm burning!" she continued to screech.

I couldn't get to her. My sister's boyfriend fell through the floor. Over the roar, I shouted to him that Kimmy was under what had been the staircase. Paul, with his clothes ripped, face blackened and covered in blood, climbed over burning debris and bricks to what was left of the staircase. I could no longer see or hear him and was suddenly completely alone.

At once, the roar seemed to weaken, debris stopped falling, and an extraordinary stillness filled the air. The light shifted inexplicably and dramatically. Within the angry burning chaos, a white-blue evanescence caught my attention. I pulled my head up from my hands to see a hole leading to more whiteness. Was it snow? Was I in hell? Was it a peek of the backyard?

White figures swirled above me. They were not just swirling, either. I heard them calling me, a sort of silent music urging me to crawl to the hole. The bricks seared my feet, but ahead the brightness made me think of heaven. I couldn't breathe. I hurt badly and I needed fresh air.

Climbing from the wreckage, I staggered forward and outside with my clothes and skin scorched into a blackened mass and smoke curling off me. Smoldering, I was still on fire.

A few weeks before I had been sitting in my fourth-grade homeroom class at St. Ambrose Catholic School, wearing my gray madras uniform over a white starched shirt with gray wool knee socks and saddle shoes.

Sister Catherine, a nun we all feared, sternly held up her boney finger to the class and said with authority, "Class, if you ever catch fire, you must roll in dirt. The dirt will put out the fire."

Now, as I was burning alive, scary Sister Catherine's recent words came to mind, but I faced another dilemma. The only dirt available was my grandparent's abundant garden behind the garage, now covered in snow. Grandpa, who like Sister Catherine was a "voice of authority," always warned us to steer clear of the garden. We would often help him plant peas, okra, beans and tomatoes. That was fine, but we were never, ever allowed to "play" in the garden.

I stood fretting that I would get in trouble for rolling in the garden, especially because I had to dig through the snow even to get to the dirt—the dirt that had this power over fire. The pain was unbearable, burning into my bones. Noticing that my skin was white and falling off, I hastily dropped to the ground, rolled in the snow and clawed for dirt underneath trying to put the fire out.

Worse, I also pressed shards of glass and debris from the house further into my skin. The pain was beyond words. People outside a catastrophe always wonder what those in extreme jeopardy are thinking. For my part, my mind groped for help from any spiritual being, a miracle worker, even Sister Catherine.

The explosion's devastation stretched throughout the yard and the neighbor's yard. As I lay in the snow-covered dirt behind the garage, I heard my name being called. Yet my mind drifted, and I imagined laughing on our boat as we cruised the Detroit River.

"Lesia! Lesia!"

"Honey! Lesia, where are you?"

It occurred to me, no one would ever find me behind the garage. I had to get to the front of the house to get help. If I didn't get up, they wouldn't see me, wouldn't hear me. The sirens and shouting continued. I just couldn't stand. I couldn't. I closed my eyes, my thoughts fading.

A small chain-link fence separated my grandparents' postage-stamp size yard from the neighbors to the rear. When we visited my grandparents, a young boy often stood at this fence and waved at us. The boy was "never right," according to my grandmother. Harmless, lonely, yet "not right."

At this moment, I opened my eyes slightly and saw him, the neighbor boy. I pulled myself up. His face was frozen with terror.

"Can you please help me?" I winced as I reached for him. He fled into his house without a word.

So the search for help continued. I stumbled back over burning debris to where the driveway had been. Was that my grandpa's car underneath the bricks and burning wood? My grandfather never let a Saturday go by without washing his car. The screams continued. My world was shattered. On the opposite side of the debris covering the car, I saw my sister, skin blackened, shouting, "Here she is, I found her … I found her … Oh, my God, I found Lesia!"

Chris is my oldest sibling, and she was often the only controlling presence in the midst of chaos at home. She was the safe one to go to when my mother was not there. Seeing Chris, who had always seemed so invincible, in a state of dishevelment, clothes torn, wounded and bleeding was stunning.

I still feel this image of Chris marked the beginning of a life that would never be the same for me, a new life outside my family's ability to rectify bad situations.

A huge mound of debris separated us. Flames were still everywhere.

"Lesia! Lesia! Come here, take my hand … take my hand … here. Just come here," Chris shouted repeatedly over the mound of wreckage.

I began to climb the rubble toward her outstretched hand. She pulled me over the burning debris. The sustained urge for survival, which is innate, burst through my head like a huge strange wave hitting the beach. The panic and adrenaline that had propelled me to this moment must have used itself up. A kind of euphoria took over. It was as though I was dreaming; everything was in slow motion.

My burns were so horrific that I was numb. My feet were cut, my clothes in shreds. I might have wanted to be held but couldn't bear to be touched. It didn't dawn on me then that my angels were cradling me.

The sounds of ambulances, fire trucks and police cars were deafening.

Whenever anyone meets a severe trauma—I think of it as being pushed down into a black airless nowhere—his or her consciousness feels a choice. This choice presents them with, on the one hand, a decision to submit, to cease to live. On the other hand, their consciousness offers them the opposite in the form of hope, the hope that for me took the form of angels.

The piercing screams of those around me reverberated in my head. My name was shouted, but I didn't answer; I was fading in and out. And my journey in and out of consciousness had only started.

I knew I was burned badly, but didn't realize how ruinous my situation was until they loaded us into the ambulance. Two dirty, sweaty firemen were attempting to coax my large statuesque grandpa into the ambulance. On either side of him, one under each of Grandpa's arms, they were trying to maneuver him. My grandpa resisted, struggling and pleading with them.

"No, no, no, I can't. My granddaughter is in my basement! I have to get Lesia! Let go of me. I have to save her!"

"Grandpa, Grandpa, I'm right here. I'm right here, Grandpa. Come get in, sit by me!"

"No," Grandpa stammered. "That's not my granddaughter … "

Was I so badly burned that he didn't recognize me? Why didn't he know me? Was he going crazy? What was happening? I looked at my hands; my skin looked like wax peeling off. I caught a glimpse of my reflection. My beautiful blonde hair was entirely gone, leaving only traces of singed Brillo pad-like tufts. No wonder Grandpa was confused.

The crowded ambulance raced away with us, a family whose lives would never be the same. A piece of our hearts had been broken, broken wide open. Chris later told me that she had peeked from the ambulance's small window as we drove away. She'd seen a van with the gas company's name on the side pull up.

About that time, my parents were about to leave our house to join us for dinner at my grandparents. Their phone rang. Someone told them there'd been a fire at Dad's parents' home. In Mom and Dad's minds, a small little kitchen fire of overcooked food got out of control.

Imagine their shock at arriving within half a mile of my grandparents' home where they were stopped by yellow caution tape, police controlling traffic, crowds of people, lights flashing and smoke everywhere. My mother's quiet gentle nature shattered; she panicked, screaming and climbing over stopped cars and barricades to reach the scene. We were already gone. When she finally got to the scene of the explosion, a fireman told her they knew I had gotten out because they found my torn clothing around a small hole in the back of the house. That's all the assurance they could give her.

The crowded emergency room of the small neighborhood hospital whirled with commotion. Everything was loud, with bright lights and people racing around.

"Why? No! Don't touch me. It hurts …, " I began to cry. "I'm OK!" I screeched. "Stop cutting my clothes off. I'm so thirsty. Please can I have something to drink? Where is my mom?"

"No, I'm sorry. Nothing to drink yet. You have been hurt," the nurse blurted. Then I reiterated the same questions and pleas … over and over again.

People were pulling, tugging, and cutting off my clothes. It was agonizing. Every touch was a fresh wound. I continued to beg anyone who would listen to give me something to drink.

My pleadings continued, "Please, please don't touch me. I hurt," I mumbled over and over again. "I just want my mom and dad. I want to be left alone. I want to go home. Can I go home now?" My mother would make it stop hurting; that's what I thought anyway.

The medication seemed to kick in, because the intense pain started to lift and I felt a little relief.

Suddenly, I heard my mother's voice down the hall.

"Mom, Mom, I'm in here." I could hear my own voice but not sure anyone else could. All I wanted to do was see my mom. I peeked through my swollen eyes to see my mother on one side of the bedside and my father on the other. They were both crying.

Deep in the midst of trauma, love presents itself in its purest form. We must have the courage to look for it, feel it. Not be afraid of it.

"Why are you guys crying?" I mumbled. This was the first time I had seen my father cry.

My mother's hand lay lightly on my chest over the sheets. I saw my father take my mother's hand and say to her, "Gloria, I love you and we're going to get through this together." Seeing my parents show love toward each other had been so rare in recent years that I knew my situation was bad. Was I dead? Dad's gesture was like a slice of heaven in the hell we were living.

An ambulance soon transported me from the small Saratoga hospital to Detroit Children's Hospital. My mother was at my side, but at each bump and turn in the road I hurt more. "Please turn the siren off," I whimpered. "It's scaring me. Where are we going, Mom? Can we go home now? Are you taking me home?" Sedation made everything even more confusing. I was thinking that if I could get home, I would stop hurting.

I spent the following weeks in a drug-induced coma. It was as if I were hyper-conscious; I could hear familiar voices even while heavily medicated. I lay in a large oxygen tent with zippers on each side. The sound of the zipper opening was a signal that pain was coming. Every part of me was in torment. "Please, don't touch me," I continued to moan.

With incessant pain, my consciousness sought a way out. One night when the pain was particularly intolerable, I felt myself drift up to the ceiling. From there, I was away from the pain and could observe my body below me in the bed. As I floated there, the same bright white light that had led the way out of the burning house appeared.

With that, an astonishing feeling of serenity blanketed me. This "familiar" tranquil white light was now everywhere. Gentle stairs appeared before me with tall figures hovering on the top stair. My vulnerable fearful thoughts vanished along with all concern for the pain. I started to climb the wide infinite staircase to reach the figures at the top.

Bathing in the serenity of pure love, I continued to climb. This is where I belong, I softly whispered to myself. I basked in this calm energy for awhile and noticed that the figures around me were communicating with me in an unspoken language. It was though I was one of them. The message wasn't in actual words, but I'll use words to describe it.

Nearly at the top, they told me to return to the small body lying in the bed.

"No, I want to stay here." I put this as a gentle request to the figure at the top of the stairs. The being gave me the clear message that this was not an option. I was to return and finish the journey of the child in the bed. "But there is a lot of pain in her," I tried to reason.

The largest of the three figures bathed in white light clarified that I must return to the little girl I was and they would surround me, encourage me, and carry me. Importantly, I was not to worry. Reinforced and feeling less lonely, I turned around and faced the familiar intense pain. There was not a word spoken. The exchange was one of pure understanding, never a misunderstanding.

The spirit world guides us when we are in our deepest pain. But it's our willingness to surrender, and open our heart in order to trust what we hear and feel.

As weeks passed I started to "come around." I woke to the sweet sound of my mother's voice. "Lesia, wake up, please wake up ..." my mother pleaded.

I couldn't see her. *Where was she?* I'd "seen" my celestial visitors, but my physical eyes hadn't seen much of anything since the induced coma.

A month before the explosion my mother and I had been Christmas shopping at Hudson's Department Store. I had spotted a long, deep cherry-red maxi coat and begged my mother to purchase it for me.

"No," she said with frustrated eyes, "we're not buying you a new coat. You have plenty of coats at home." Being the youngest of five children, I always received hand-me-downs from my older sisters. There was never a new coat for the youngest.

A typical little girl, I pestered my mother about that coat for days. With five children, no viable means of support, and a husband who was always gone, there was no way she could indulge me with a coat like that.

Now, Mom pleaded, "Lesia honey, please wake up. Open your eyes." Peeking through crusted bandages I saw a room full of get-well cards, stuffed animals, soft toys, and hand written letters taped to my bed. They looked as though they had been there for weeks.

My eyes, to the extent they could even open, were full of my mother, who stood at the foot of my bed holding the red maxi coat. Tears streaked down her cheeks. I honestly don't know what was more beautiful, the coat or her. As a transition, this awakening from the "coma" delivered me to Mom, Dad and siblings, but it also came with agonizing and unrelenting rehab.

Having burns on more than half of my body, I thought I had experienced the worst pain ever. That was before my "tub room" treatments started. The nurse drew warm water into a white porcelain tub, inside of which she placed a round, stainless steel cylinder-like machine that made the water turbulent.

The idea was to loosen up dead burned skin that had melted into my flesh. What skin didn't come off from the turbulent water was subjected to a wiry scrub brush to "help it along." It was excruciating.

The tub room was directly across the hall from the burn ward, one room of six beds, all occupied by children who were seriously burned. My bed was number six, the closest to the door and nearest to the tub room. Every morning after breakfast the treatments began. A nurse took the child from bed one first. Within minutes I heard the blood-curdling screams, the endless pleading, crying for the treatment to stop. In time, the nurse brought the child back to his or her bed with clean bandages. The child always whimpered in pain with a popsicle to sooth the trauma of the daily tub room experience. Then it was bed two, then three. By the time it came to me, I was petrified with fear from listening to the screams of previous children—and still not yet recovered from yesterday's tub treatment.

Learning to go to another place in my mind was my means of coping. The daily agony forced me to try and go back to the light—the same light that got me out of the house, the same light that saturated the stairs with the angelic figures. Often my sister Chris accompanied me to the tub room, mostly to cajole me into allowing the nurses to scrub off the dead skin with the brushes. "Just a few more scrubs and we'll be done," they lied.

During these horrific treatments I always found the darting nurses' eyes and begged them to stop scrubbing:

"PLEASE, don't do this to me," I pleaded. I wanted to die, everyday. The tub experience happened on a daily basis for weeks until the wounds were at last outside the risk of infection.

All this was in the sixties. Today the tub room treatments persist. If I hear crying from a child that I can't see, I have to stop what I'm doing, find the child and confirm that they are not being tortured. Here on the healing side, I have moved past the horrific experience and can now enjoy a soothing hot bubble bath.

Teaching myself to go to the familiar angelic light during my desperate escape from traumatic situations became a meditation the rest of my life—a gift of serenity anytime I need it. Which of your childhood gifts do you still utilize today? Make a list. They are there. Have you forgotten?

Christmas was approaching. Nurses showed up with Santa pins on their uniforms and stuffed reindeers. My mother brought me a beautiful small silver imitation Christmas tree.

Even with all the joy of the season, I felt like giving up. Between the tub treatments, the crying children in my room, more tears and pain, the constant intrusion of forced feedings, needling, nurses pushing me to sit up, stand up, walk, I was desperate for any escape—even death.

Then there was the loss of my family, namely the restricted visits from my grandparents. My parents felt (rightly so, I would soon realize) that my grandparents—who had lost everything and were deeply vulnerable themselves—should not suffer the additional distress of seeing my wounds. Still this loss was devastating. Yes, I was giving up.

My family thought that coming home for Christmas day might cheer me up. Wouldn't seeing our house, being with our whole family together, and presents encourage me to heal? Getting dressed to go home meant putting on my red maxi coat over my hospital gown and bulky bandages and dressings. Preposterous and difficult, it hardly seemed worth it. My bandaged hands didn't fit through the sleeves. Those on my back and shoulders made me look hunchback. But I was wearing my new coat.

Attendants pushed my wheelchair into the old rusty elevators to ground level. Every movement seemed loud. But the blast of cold fresh air soothed the perpetual burning of my skin, but nothing prepared me for the staring of the crowds on the street as I was loaded into our car—going home for the day. The looks were all aghast and shocked. The best of them were sad, looks of pity, but they also included horror and revulsion.

This was just the beginning of my life in a new body. I was no longer that cute, shy, happy little blonde girl who always got smiles. The silent stares from strangers were just as hurtful. Did they think I couldn't see them?

At home I lay in bandages on the couch. My pain was familiar and unabating. Every time I opened my eyes, I'd catch glimpses of people peering around the corner to see if I was OK.

"Is she asleep?" Mom whispered. My neighborhood friend Jenny Lou came over but was afraid to look at me. "Just peek around the corner," I heard my sister say. My family was just as terrified about my being home as I was. Much later my sister shared that bringing me home was not a good idea, but they were desperate for me to heal.

Back at the hospital, I was relieved. It felt like my new home. There I wasn't an anomaly. Everyone was ill and in discomfort. I fit in. The hospital was a place where I felt consistency. My new normal. That relief only lasted until the following day when another round of tub scrubbings, bandage changes and procedures resumed.

Meanwhile, I played with a large rubber bouncy ball in the hallways, and felt a bit stronger. I bonded with the nurses. They too were angels, so fresh from heaven I would watch as they tried to hide their "wings." One nurse, her blonde hair up in a high bun, had soft eyes and a gentle voice. She seemed to float in and out of my room and always apologized when she had to change my dressings, because she knew it inflicted intense pain. I could see the love and compassion in her face, daily. I watched the clock for 3 p.m. when she started her night shift and dreaded weekends when she was off. Her gentle energy contrasted with another nurse whose bedside manner reflected frustration and little patience.

Clearly, my blonde angel liked her job much more than my frustrated angel whose wing seemed broken.

My mother's visit was the high point of every day. Arriving at 10 a.m. when visiting hours opened, she always brought my favorites—frozen strawberries and Fritos corn chips.

Many days I looked at her through my bandages and thought how exhausted she looked. Once, as I was drifting off to sleep, my father arrived. He thought I was asleep.

"Gloria, you look very tired. You need to go home. Lesia will be OK; I will stay with her. It's OK. We have all been through so much and besides you have four other children at home who need you," Dad said.

"I can't leave her, Don. She won't eat unless I'm here," my mother wept.

"Gloria, go home. Get some rest," my father insisted.

My father's words struck me. I was only nine, but all of a sudden I understood that I wasn't the only one suffering, that my suffering was hurting others. That moment shifted something big within me. As I fought to stop the silent tears behind my bandages I made a decision to protect Mom, not to let her feel any more pain from my accident. I remembered seeing her laugh before the accident but not since. I needed to work on my humor, for her.

The price we pay to protect those we love seems worth it—still does.

This overheard conversation was one of the defining moments when I resolved to do my best to hide pain and build courage, to get through this journey under my own steam alone with my angels. In a way, the accident was a call to duty. I needed to get my family through this; they were a mess.

CHAPTER THREE

Sinking

At any moment's notice,
one's life can change.

The hospital released me in early spring, three months after the accident. Home was the first major adjustment. I alone was physically damaged, but clearly my whole family had been traumatized. Their internal suffering was apparent. Darting eyes, full of fear. Worried looks frozen on guilt-ridden faces. Siblings resentful because I got all the attention, which pushed aside their own needs. We all suffered in our own way. My family still suffers today.

It wasn't as if there was a mutually agreed upon game plan. Communication between all of us was strained, at best. Add in other dynamics like alcoholism and an unstable financial picture, and we were all grasping for handholds moment by moment, trying to hold off the drama. At least I was. The others tried to protect me, but didn't know how. How could they? And whatever coping strategy they had was improvised behind the scenes, making me feel even more excluded. We were lost!

One would think when a family goes through a tragedy—such as a big accident like mine, the death of a family member, the job loss of the major breadwinner, or even forfeiting a home—that the family members would cleave together, pool resources and support each other. Sadly, the opposite is the norm. Whatever is going on behind the scenes, the stuff we all try to bury gets magnified on the other side of a tragedy. My family was no different.

"Mom told us that we were not allowed to stare at you," my sister Chris told me much later. "But we would come and peek in while you were sleeping." Of course, I knew on some level that this was going on, that my physical appearance had become both a forbidden topic and attraction.

When we were out in public, people stared. My family never acknowledged the staring or said anything back to the person. We would shuffle along or out the door. I felt like such a spectacle; I hated my life.

Being in the company of my grandparents was an entirely different nightmare. Whereas Grandpa handled my situation gingerly, Grandma was a fountain of discomfort. They had tremendous guilt, particularly my grandmother. At least she was the one who showed it.

I dreaded going out with her in public, because when people stared, she put her arm around me and began to cry, "Ain't it awful? My poor granddaughter, look how burned she is." Once Grandma had an onlooker hooked, she continued to weep, "My house burned down. We lost everything." I wanted to crawl under the clothes rack, the vegetable stand, anywhere to hide.

She was in such deep pain. I'd step in, "It's OK, Grandma, I'm all right. Let's go home." I longed to run to the car, and sometimes I did, dragging her with me. Often the person would feed into the story and follow us, asking question after question: "Well, what happened? Is your whole house gone? How badly is she burned?" With that my grandmother, buried in sorrow, would pull up my shirt, baring my scars for the stranger's gawking and commentary.

The next hurdle was the inevitability of my return to school. There were whispers behind closed doors. "I'm afraid to send her to school because I know the kids will stare at her and tease her," I heard my mother say to her friend on the phone. I sank against the wall in the next room, trying to disappear.

What was I expecting? A family meeting to plan my return to school? For Dad or Mom to say, "Let's talk about our next step as a family?" Everyone was so tense and irritable that even mundane topics such as "what's for dinner?" were charged. Anyway, I already had more attention than I wanted. *My reactions were normal* and so were those of my family members. Each clinging to their ways of coping—sadness, sense of victimhood, helplessness, and alcohol. My family was no different.

One day, as my mother was ironing, I found the courage to broach the subject. "Mom, I think I'm ready to go back to school." I saw my mother shoot a glance to my older sister with a look of terror.

"Oh well, I don't know, Lesia. I'll call the school next week."

A few minutes later I overheard her mumble to my sister, "My God, Chris, what are we going to do?"

Then rallying to bail out my mother and lessen her fear, I said with confidence, "Yep, Mom, I'm ready to go back to school, but I only want to go part-time." In my mind it was fair. I needed to test the waters in the classroom and on the playground. I didn't share my protective strategy but I felt sure I could handle school if only part-time, no matter how bad it might be.

Besides, I needed to stay close to home to make sure nothing else crazy happened like another explosion. This may sound ridiculous, but I honestly felt that my family needed my good instincts to stay safe. I'd been the one to feel anxiety at my grandparents' house before the explosion.

> *Whatever happens to a child, or any member of the family, happens to the entire family. Whether we acknowledge it at the time, the hurt is there and will eventually surface. The more thoroughly and more honestly we strive to heal the easier the recovery, but all parties must be willing.*

Clearly, no one else's instincts had been able to protect me, let alone themselves.

My mother had a quiet wisdom about her. She was emotionally beaten down by the uncertainty of the constant crises by this point, but occasionally—like this time—the wisdom would surface. She looked at me and said, "If you are ready to go back to school, Lesia, you must go full-time."

Returning to school was horrific.

The staring and taunting was intolerable. Nobody was prepared. I certainly wasn't prepared. The school wasn't prepared and neither were the students, nor the nuns.

A few days back into my fourth grade class at St. Ambrose, Sister Catherine, in full nun regalia called me to the front of the class and said to the students, "This is why you shouldn't play with matches." This was my first deep experience of humiliation among my classmates. The injustice of it. How could the same nun who directed that I roll in dirt to save my life say something so unfair and demoralizing?

To be objectified, to be treated as if I didn't have feelings or consciousness, was searing. Gone forever was the fail-safe cover of fitting in. No more being invisible. No more speedy retort that made everything OK. Everything required explanation.

I whispered softly back to the nun, "But I wasn't playing with matches."

After this humiliating experience, I shuffled back to my chair and sank behind my desk. I didn't know what to do. I didn't know where to turn. I desperately needed help and there was none there, so I turned to my angels. I had to believe there was a better place for me, that my calamity had happened for a reason that would eventually sort itself out. The angels were my only option.

The day dragged on with continued teasing on the playground. No way could I go home and tell my mom, dad or siblings about my experience at school that day. It would only bring them more pain. I convinced myself that I could suck it up and get through it on my own. Besides, what could my family do? *Nothing.* I was strong enough, wasn't I? I had survived the explosion and grueling tub treatments in the burn unit.

Remembering the beams of light shining on the stairs as well as those that led me out of the burning house and the angels' promise to surround me, I felt I could get through school. Those moments of strength came and went, and in the meantime, I improvised.

My usual weekday routine was to begin the day with feigning a stomach ache, begging my mother to let me stay home. I fine-tuned my ability to convince her that I "didn't feel well," because it was less charged than saying, "Mom, kids are teasing me at school." I would lie in bed holding my stomach pleading with her as she leaned in the doorway with arms folded, "Lesia, you have to go to school," she pleaded. "The truant officer will come to the door."

My mother had to be in such pain to watch her precious child suffer in sadness as she held her ground. Then the bargaining would start: "How about if you go to school, and

I'll take you shopping afterwards?" she'd ask. Well, I knew this wouldn't happen because we had no money. That particular line of seduction never worked. "Lesia, I need to drive the other kids to school. When I return, please be ready to go," she'd insist before walking down the stairs, head hung.

My classmates weren't verbally confrontational, maybe because I wasn't verbal back, but in the background I heard myself referred to as a "monster" and "freak." Of course, this took a toll. More painful than words was the exclusion and isolation. I ate lunch by myself. I was picked last for any sports. I walked alone in the halls. This social disenfranchisement was more agonizing than the taunts. "There's the burned girl; she was playing with matches," the whispers continued daily.

Gym class was the worst. Being catholic-school students, we all had to change into our gym uniforms. On gym days, I often wrapped my hand in gauze I kept in my locker, in order to feign an injury. This was my M.O. for staying in my clothes so no one could see that I had horrendous scars on my back and stomach too.

After the accident I tried to re-establish my relationships with the neighborhood friends, but it was difficult. The world looked different to me now. There was one school friend who invited me somewhere and said she would sit near me, but I was in such a state of uncertainty that I couldn't bring myself to accept these overtures.

Fear had lodged in me. My most stable foundation, my grandparents' house and their own security, had been ripped out from underneath us and had forever changed my family and, in particular, me. Everyday I'd wrestle with anxiety. *What is to prevent my own home from blowing up? What is to stop our car from blowing up? What is to stop the school bus from blowing up? I already hurt now.* What is to prevent it from getting worse?

People can walk through a lifetime without confronting a sense of "the unknown," the reality that any moment one's whole life can change. Doing so at the age of nine was a lot to handle, to think about, and now to live with. In addition to the overwhelming loneliness, my other prevailing feeling was daunting dread.

The year following the explosion created more chaos for my family. Burn injuries, liabilities, gas company's fault, tears, no money, too much money, hating school, and displaced grandparents—trauma tore at the thin threads that wove my family together. I felt as alone in this journey as I did at school. My family was supportive but they were also ravaged. We were in survival mode—as though we were the walking wounded—walking under a roof that "leaked" when it rained, thinking we were staying dry. Whether from tears or from a storm, our situation was leaking constantly at every seam.

There were trips back to the hospital for minor physical therapy,

In the thick of trauma we have a choice—a choice to put our trust in the serenity of the moment or to allow our fear to consume us. The former feels a lot better and is ultimately much more productive.

surgeries to be scheduled, and assessments of my future including medical evaluations, which always involved stripping down for strange doctors with cameras. Take teenage insecurity and modesty about body development, and then add a layer of gruesome scaring, with unceasing invitations to prying eyes.

A lawsuit was well underway. My mother was my silent strength. My father was the handsome, funny, charismatic one—the showman. I needed both of them. They needed my strength too and my angels.

I walked in on many hushed discussions as well as loud arguments about the pending lawsuit. My father hired lawyers to watch our lawyers. Representing us against Consumers Power Company was the legal firm of Hoffa and Chodak. Yes, Jimmy Hoffa's brother was my father's choice of attorney; nothing was ever straight and clear with my father. My mother silently followed his lead unless her children were clearly at risk.

"Not 'no,' but *hell no*, Don." My mother stood before my father. "You are *not* putting our daughter on the witness stand in this trial, no. I will *not* let that happen. She has been through enough."

It was one of the rare times my father surrendered to my mother's wisdom.

More often, Dad got his own way. We spent the summer after the explosion in Miami on a yacht my father purchased, traded into or acquired—we never knew which. Her name was "Safari." She was an 83-foot Mathis, built in

1934. Such a beautiful yacht. Docked behind a hotel in Miami, we swam in the hotel pool, ate at the employees' buffet (another of my father's "deals") in a garage by the docks, and rode the hotel elevators when we could get away with it.

My father flew back and forth from Miami to Detroit with a few side trips to the Caribbean in between.

It was my first summer in a swimsuit with my scars. I swam with a t-shirt over my bathing suit to hide my injured skin. It was easier than explaining to the hotel guests, employees and random people walking by what happened to me. The scars on my face I couldn't hide—except under an ugly hat that kept out the burning sun. At night I surrendered to lowering my head, facing away and praying they didn't stop to ask.

The worst was children's reactions, because they were unrestrained. When a child walked into my vicinity, they frequently made loud questions that then precipitated even more painful commentary.

"Eww, Mommy, what's on her face?" the child would blurt out.

"Shh, don't look at her face," the mother would reply.

"But Mommy, she's ugly. I'm scared … Mommy pick me up." The child would then begin to cry.

"But Mommy, but why … her face is so ugly. I hate it, Mommy."

It never seemed to stop.

Both the parent and I hunted frantically for an escape.

Other times, such as in an elevator with no escape, I tried to turn away, burying myself. If I were lucky and fast, I'd be facing another direction before the child noticed me, staving off a punishing interaction.

Do you know how many children vacation in Miami with their families in the summer? It seemed like millions.

My entire being was on "high alert" avoiding unknown children. There were so many fraught occasions. Let's say I was sitting with family and their friends and someone mentioned, "Say, have you seen Edith's little boy? He is growing up. I invited her over to swim and told her to bring the kids. She is bringing a friend too. They will be here soon."

Danger! Danger! I'd whisper to myself. As soon as the car pulled up, I'd slip out the back door to avoid an uncomfortable and devastating line of questions, plus bad behavior from the children. Often the reactions from the parents were just as damaging.

"Sweetie, just don't look at her."

"Yes, honey, I know she is ugly but she can't help it."

"Yes, honey, she is not as pretty as you."

"I know, baby, but it is not polite to stare."

"She was probably playing with matches. See, you should never play with matches."

"Stay away from her. I don't know if it is contagious."

Dispirited, I watched and listened to the parents struggle—or worse if I was with friends and a new child came around—the child's behavior put everyone on edge. Then everyone would look to see what I would say, how I would react ...

I wanted so badly to disappear. Going to a community pool was out of the question as were camps, school activities or any group function where there would be children.

I did *everything* to cover my scars. Mostly, avoidance was my choice of protection. Daily challenges, big and small, were constant. Given the adventurous nature of my family, there was always someone going somewhere—so I could pick and choose. My sister Chris took me under her wing, and enfolded me into her group of high school friends. I felt safe there. She became a protector in many ways for me, inviting me to school outings and events. But let's face it: a high school senior didn't want a ten-year-old hanging around, scars or no scars.

Before my injury, my sister was a cheerleader at a Catholic high school. She was dating the star football player and they had made me a mascot. Just a year before, I had waved pom-poms high in the air while sitting on her shoulders. How I wished I could again feel my innocent life.

We returned to Detroit after my first summer as a "burned girl." Chris announced she and the star football player were getting married. I was to be the flower girl. My excitement was crushed when I saw the bridesmaid dresses. Mine was to match all the bridesmaids; it was sleeveless with a scoop back.

"What about my dress for the wedding, Mom?" I whispered. "All my scars on my back and arm will show …"

"It's OK, Lesia. The seamstress will put fabric on the back to cover your scars." Staring at my worried expression, she added, "You can wear a hat too if you'd like." My mom cringed.

"A hat in church? Mom, I can't wear a hat in church! Are the other girls wearing hats?"

The wedding was a turning point in my life. Music was blaring during the reception in the parish hall. I stood on the side and I could feel my body wanting to move, to feel joy, to be normal. There it was, "Jeremiah was a bullfrog ... was a good friend of mine ..." Going with the feeling, I jumped into the dance floor and let it rip. I danced until my feet had blisters. I could feel the love and laughter coming from everyone.

"Look at you! You're dancing! You're an awesome dancer ..."

Something inside me changed that evening. I crawled into bed with a smile on my face. The corners of my mouth rising up, feeling that maybe I was going to be OK.

I had been evaluated by Reed Dingman, MD, from the University of Michigan, Ann Arbor's Burn Center. I had grown respectful of doctors, seeing so many over the past year. Perhaps I was in awe of the steady fatherly figure. They were so different than my father. Dr. Dingman sent me to consult with Dr. Ralph Millard, a renown reconstructive surgeon whose offices were in Miami, alongside Jackson Memorial Hospital. My mother and I made a

We are in charge. We teach people how to treat us. When I brought attention to my scars and my wounds so did everyone else. I began to learn when I acted as if I "looked" normal, so did other people—eventually.

few visits to Dr. Millard's office to discuss a plan for "fixing" my face.

One could tell Dr. Millard was an important man, because he always had a retinue of men and women in white doctor coats trailing him, and he had famous peoples' pictures and awards hanging floor-to-ceiling in the halls of his offices.

There were several private entrances and exits to his office, all for the rich and famous, I assumed, until one day after my most recent surgery. So bandaged up that only my mouth and one eye peeked through, I sat in the waiting room. In shuffled a little boy with a contorted face—nearly monster-like. We shared a quick glance, then a safe small smile. I was glad we were not in those private waiting rooms. Seeing this boy I suddenly felt I was not alone.

Dr. Millard was a magic man who could fix anyone's face, I was learning. Another of my living angels, he was the closest thing next to God in my mind. I knew that little boy felt the same. I could see it in his eye, between the crusty gauze.

Summer ended and we drove back to Detroit. Winter was approaching; my grandparents were unhappy living in an apartment coping with the loss of everything. My parents' nightclub continued to be a huge success, and I needed to begin the long journey of reconstructive surgery in Miami.

"Let's move to Florida," my father announced in October.

"What?" My mother was stunned. "What about the kids' school? It's the middle of their semester, Don!" I just got them all registered in school … then there is the house we'll need to pack up and sell. And what about our nightclub?"

My father dismissed her concerns saying, "You worry too much," and left the room.

A week later my father announced that he had sold the nightclub and bought a nice Fort Lauderdale home on a canal, big enough for all of us. He asked my mother to pack up the car with enough belongings for a few weeks. The idea was for Mom to take Darrin and me, the youngest, while Danny and Cindy stayed with my grandparents in Detroit so they could finish the high school year. Chris was now married to Paul.

My father said he'd hire movers to pack up everything and join us in Florida as soon as possible. We believed him.

My mother, Darrin, and I drove to our new life in Fort Lauderdale. My father was right. The house was beautiful, right on the canal. A few weeks later, my father called from a pay phone on the road to say he was only two hours away. Thrilled, we stood on the curb, waiting for the movers to bring all our furniture, dishes, clothes, linens and treasures. Everything we owned was finally going to be here, plus Dad.

I was giddy with anticipation about decorating my new bedroom with my Snoopy posters, stuffed animals, lava lamps, personal treasures and pictures of the few friends I had. In another example of how I'd "stuffed" my feelings, I had not yet read the hundreds of get-well cards and letters that I had received when I was in the hospital.

As a family we stuffed everything, particularly anything painful. And we found humor in the coping, if we could. After all these months, though, I felt ready to look at the accident, and anticipating those cards symbolized that readiness. I remember seeing the tattered paper grocery bags of get-well cards my mom had brought from the hospital to the house. Now they would be arriving! It would take me a long time to look at all of them, but I was finally ready to read!

My father pulled up beeping the horn of his new pickup truck pulling a tarp-covered trailer. We all ran outside.

"He's here!" we all squealed.

"How was your drive down, Dad? When will the movers get here?" We peppered him with questions.

"Look what I bought you and Darrin," Dad answered evasively, throwing back the tarp to display two new Honda 70 mini-bikes. I picked the blue; Darrin got the red.

"The moving truck will be here in an hour," he mumbled.

Sometime later a small U-Haul truck pulled up with two small barrels of old miscellaneous stuff from the house— stuff that meant nothing to us, junk.

"Don, there has been a mistake!" my mother cried. "Where are all our things?"

My father assumed his all-to-predictable defensiveness, then dismissively explained that we needed to start fresh, make a clean slate for the future. Yep, he had sold everything. What he didn't sell, he gave away and then tossed the rest, my get-well cards included. Everything—my mother's family china, wedding gifts, pictures, clothes, furniture, our baby memorabilia, photo albums, kitchen pans, and silverware ... the entire contents of a four-bedroom and three-bath home—was gone.

Thus for the second time in my young life, I experienced what it felt like to lose everything—stability, possessions and most importantly trust in my father to make good decisions for the family. My priorities and my safety were again my responsibility alone. I learned that physically hugging myself to sleep was better than any Snoopy poster. My angels once again scooped me up and whispered to me in the tiniest of moments.

Loss is the harshest reminder that self worth, faith, and richness of life are not in possessions but in the healing that follows.

Dad declared that we were going to buy everything we needed, new. My mother sat on the curb and wept. In my memory, that moment marked their final emotional severance. My mother and father didn't speak much after that, at least not with any devotion, respect or eye contact. Yet somehow I really enjoyed riding that mini-bike.

My older siblings in Detroit moved into my grandparents' rental to complete the school year. After the year was over, they all joined us at our new home in Florida. My grandparents flew down and moved into the separate apartment upstairs of our new house on the canal. One big happy dysfunctional family, ready to launch more drama.

It was time to go back to school. The pit in my stomach grew. I'd been dreading yet another school full of mocking children, a brand new school. Then she returned with the news.

"Lesia, the nice Catholic school not far from here is full and not accepting new students now."

For a nanosecond I was elated: No school for me! No Teasing! No Staring! Woo-hoo!

She continued, "So I had to register you at the local public school. You start Monday."

My heart sank. Public school meant classmates who were even nastier and tougher.

"Oh. OK, Mom. So no uniforms?" I was trying to act normal. "When can we go shopping for school clothes?" I asked, but before she could answer, I was gone.

I ran to my room, threw myself on my bed and smothered my tears, hiding my terror from my mother, protecting her, again. It was a rough weekend, learning that my father had heaved all our possessions and that my scars and I must face a new school in two days—and a public school at that.

My worry skyrocketed: *Would gym class require me to change clothes where everyone would see the scars on my back? What would my first day be like?* Sunday afternoon came and I started to get the familiar stomachache.

My siblings were already registered. Why did my sister Cindy love school so much? She was always coming home with tons of books and her "A" homework where teachers often wrote "excellent" across the top. To make matters worse she was actually pushing for a perfect attendance record.

My brother Darrin was very shy but cute as measured by teenagers of the seventies. Girls flocked to him. It helped that my father let Darrin drive his sports cars and taught him his charming ways. Danny developed a crush on the girl down the street. I could tell marriage was coming. I had hoped I wasn't picked to be a flower girl again, the dress incident trickled back.

Then there was my situation: Fear, hatred, and sometimes nausea. Even the thought of going to school sent me into a tailspin of excuses as to why I couldn't possibly go.

Monday came. I got dressed slowly and dragged myself to the car with my new book bag in tow. Mom and I arrived at the school and slowly shuffled to the office for check in. It was an old two story building, paint chipping off the front wall, dead grass everywhere. Kids were hanging around.

My head went down, dodging stares, as we headed for the front door, the one with the paint chipping off. Inside, dark wooden floors reinforced my gloom. Each step I made seemed louder. My catholic schools had been well maintained. This place seemed broken; so was I.

"Oh, this must be Lesia," said a nice lady behind an old wooded desk in the office.

"Yes, we're here to check her in for her first day," my mom said. I was very busy keeping my head low, but I knew my mom was standing next to me watching me. I just wanted to get through this without inflicting any more pain on my mother so I faked a smile.

Paperwork took longer than expected, the bell had rung and I could hear kids rushing to class, and then sounds in the hall diminished. Dang, I thought, considering what would happen next. By then all the kids were in class, the teacher had begun, and this lady was still shuffling papers, talking to my mom.

This meant that my entrance into my first class would be disruptive, all eyes on me. Middle of the school year, middle of the class—*could it get any worse?* As my mother and the lady walked me to my classroom, I fought the nausea.

"What time will you pick me up, Mom?" I whispered.

"I'll be here as soon as you get out at 2:15," she said smiling. "You'll be fine and I'm sure you'll make some friends."

The door opened, my mother gave me a little hug, then she and the lady turned to leave.

"Welcome," said a full-figured teacher in large flowery dress. She shook my hand then stood me in front of the class with her pudgy hands flapping over me. "Class, we have a new student. This is her first day, please welcome Lisa, er um is it "Leeesha? Dear, how do you pronounce your first name?" This always happens to me with my name.

"Lisa," I whispered. "It's just spelled funny." I took a chance and looked up at the class hoping for a smile from someone. All eyes on me, a few gasps and sounds of awe, no hint of a smile yet.

"Well, welcome, honey. Now go sit down over there." The teacher pointed to an empty desk in row one. Suddenly the bell rang and all jumped up and pushed through the door to their next classroom. I followed, hoping to fit in, somewhere with someone.

I made it through the day with fears that this was the way school life was going to be, forever. I lay in bed later that night, wondering if it needed to be so daunting. If my sister was pushing for the perfect attendance record, there had to be something good about school. Yet, she didn't have scars crawling on her face.

My thoughts ping-ponged. Maybe if I pretended I didn't have scars, others might forget them too. Could I really just pretend? Could I really ignore my burns? I needed to try. I was desperate to get through the school year without telling my parents how tough school was—hurting my family more.

The next day was the test of my courage. I tried forgetting I had scars and focused on being nice to the girls around me. I was slowly discovering that the friendlier I was to other girls, the nicer they were in return. It was a simple lesson. The day seemed to be over sooner than I had dreaded. I was on to something.

I was still very young—only eleven—but I observed that the way I acted became like a mirror, meaning that whatever behavior I exuded came back to me, as dependable as clock-work. I tested this approach again and again. When I acted like a victim, they treated me like a victim. When I acted nice, the kids were nice to me. I had almost convinced myself that the kids weren't just acting nice but were nice. Then a girl named Elaine arrived.

I'd not met Elaine before, but the other kids knew her. When I arrived in homeroom one morning, there she was sitting at the desk in front of me. "Hi," I said as I slipped into my desk.

She turned slightly, seemed surprised and smiled gently back. That was when I saw Elaine's teeth. They went every which way and she wore braces. Wow, she looked different than anyone I'd ever seen before. Plus, Elaine was the tallest person in the classroom, by far. She also had an odd odor and gangly gait. A lot of challenges.

"Hi," she said back, with traces of saliva spewing on my books. Class began. All was quiet until the teacher excused herself for a few minutes after giving us a reading assignment. That's when the crossfire started.

Pencil erasers, spit balls, small pieces of chalk came flying across the room at Elaine followed by targeted teasing, particularly from the boys in the back.

"Take that, Elaine … 'cause you're so ugly. Yeah, and you smell too!" came shouts from the back of the room. It was like a wild mob.

I was shocked yet relieved their cruel gibes weren't aimed at me. I sank further behind her. Most of our classmates detached from me, with only a few girls who would ask limited questions like, "Do you have a pencil I can borrow?" or "What page are we on?" The same few would stand with me at the playground. Almost friends. But poor Elaine. Whoa, they terrorized her.

I didn't know what to do to help Elaine. I had my own survival tactics to work on. The more paraphernalia they threw at her, the more she hollered back at them. I was frozen. It was a special edition of watching my theory of "how you behave comes back at you" enacted. Finally, our teacher returned and the abuse stopped, until the next time we were alone. The teacher heard the rustling in the class but ignored it.

"How was school today?" my mother asked as usual when she picked me up afterwards.

"Oh, fine," I lied and changed the subject.

Days pressed into weeks. I continued feigning stomachaches, more failed attempts at bargaining with my mom to let me stay home from school. I lost all battles. I'm sure it was just as hard for my mother to watch me drag to school as it was for me.

Yet once there at school I was dedicated to pretending there was nothing wrong with my face. I tried to act normally; hold my head up and smile. The more I acted normal—the more my classmates would treat me normal, the more I smiled and was friendly, the more friendly people were to me.

Maybe it was Elaine who took the attention away. Either way, I was both grateful that I wasn't she and saddened for her. I felt her pain.

About the time I was accepting my hated new school, an unusual smell began wafting in the open windows during math class. I began to look around; the other students seemed oblivious. I couldn't concentrate. The smell grew stronger. Something was burning! As soon as the bell rang, I dashed out the school doors racing in a panic yet trying to stay calm, looking for my mother's car. It was always a problem when being picked up. I never knew what type of car she would be driving, thanks to my father's dealings. At last, I spotted her. Running for the car, my heart wept inside. I needed to feel safe.

"Mom, what's that smell?" I shouted as I ran to her, trying not to cause her any alarm or pain in showing her I was so upset.

"Oh THAT weird smell, outside? Lesia, there is a forest fire in the Everglades swamp. I saw it on the news," she seemed calm, but with my mother you never knew what was brewing underneath.

"How far is the Everglades?" I could feel myself panicking.

"Oh, don't worry. It's quite a ways away. It's swampland."

"But Mom, look, there is so much haze in the air."

"Lesia, I see it. Lesia, not to worry. It's far away," she dimly smiled.

I worried, though. You bet I worried. The following day it was hard to pretend that I wasn't burned when the talk around school and in the classrooms was all about the big Everglades fire. My stomachaches were going to be in full swing tomorrow. *I was not coming back to school,* I vowed. *Ever.*

Though, of course, I did. That smell and the Everglades fire lasted for weeks. The horrible odor—a symbol of devastation and chaos—permeated me, disturbed my already thin hold, and with it horrible memories of terrible pain surfaced in me.

CHAPTER FOUR

Pushed Into Purpose

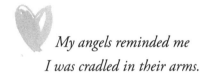

My angels reminded me
I was cradled in their arms.

$\mathbf{As}$ we were settling into our new home with no possessions and the relationship between our parents disintegrating, my father arranged to have Safari, the yacht we had lived on the previous summer in Miami, docked behind the house. Even though the entire contents of our house in Michigan were gone, amazingly we still had Safari nine months later.

Dad's passions continued. He began "acquiring" beautiful vintage yachts, a Chinese junk, a tugboat, and eventually a small barge, upon which he had a custom bar built. These vessels were tied up three deep in the narrow canal, along with a speedboat for Darrin. Our neighbors couldn't help but observe that we were *unique,* again.

The bar sitting on top of the barge was quite the gathering place on a daily basis. Dad had it built to ship to Providenciales in the Turks and Caicos Islands. It was to float against an old ship that had crashed on a reef, with the idea that customers could sit at the open floating bar, and as they pondered life, watch the sea life take residence in the sunken ship. Dad was to hire two natives to shuttle the passengers back and forth from the beach in skiffs.

The plan was brilliant. Yet my father was easily distracted. He shipped the bar, fully stocked with booze and provisions, yet he forgot to apply for the proper permits to open a bar on the island. The bar operated along the sunken treasure, yet he couldn't accept money for the booze. He gave it all away.

Late one afternoon my father pulled up at our Fort Lauderdale home in yet another unrecognizable car. He got out with a woolly monkey on his shoulder.

"Dad! What is that?" we squealed.

"Honey, it's for you! I saw her in a pet shop and fell in love." His eyes sparkled.

"What shall we name her?" I asked.

"I already did. Her name is Beatrice, after your grandmother," he smiled.

My mother walked out the front door, took one look at the monkey and sighed, "Good grief, where did you get that?"

We had Beatrice for three years. My father had a large cage built on the seawall where she swung and chirped all day long—that is when she wasn't riding on my grandfather's shoulders during his puttering around the yard.

It's not far to the circus when you are the circus.

My grandmother hated that monkey. During the chaos of boats tied up behind us, with boat captains and deck crews coming and going, I was having reconstruction on my face. My sister Cindy was beautiful; that attracted its own throng of men at the house.

It was spring break from school, a place I hated. My mother and I were in the car driving to the hospital in Miami for another surgery when I looked over at the car traveling next to us. It was a brief moment, yet time enough for me to draw comparisons of our situations on that particular day. Here was a smiling girl about my age in the car, her mother driving. Since it was school-break time, I figured they were headed somewhere really cool or fun like the mall or beach. Here I was in the car with my Mom, and I was going to be stuck and probed and cut.

Afterward, I'd recover not from some teenage caper but alone in bandages. The self-pity quietly rolled in like a weather system.

All teen years are emotionally tricky, but mine were filled with reconstructive surgeries. Every vacation involved a stay at Jackson Memorial Hospital in Miami for a series of skin grafts. I felt alone and fearful but an upcoming surgery came with a gift. It was the one time I got to go shopping with my mother … for new pajamas.

This became a ritual—something to look forward to on the doorstep of the impending pain of yet another surgery. On the way to the hospital, the familiar *why me?* feeling blanketed me. So many times, I contemplated the end to all this, an escape hatch of death, some way to finish my life. Thing was, I associated death with those angels I'd seen in my grandparents' basement. And I'd seen them again at the "portals to death"—that ascending staircase I'd seen in the hospital. To get to death, I'd have to negotiate with those angels, and thinking of them reminded me of their love and encouragement.

So, my despair, though recurring, never seemed to last for long. My angels somehow squeezed in the seat beside me in the car that day. They reminded me that I was cradled in their arms, carrying me into a life I was designed to live. I felt a load lift from my shoulders and a smile cross my face. No fear or pain could ever compare to the pure, intense love my angels brought me, ever.

A week after my surgery, where skin had been grafted to one side of my face, my parents threw a backyard barbecue. Food was grilling. There were cocktails and music. A football was being thrown about. Suddenly, while I sat in my lawn chair observing the festivities, the football came charging at my face. I had no time to protect what was under my bandages.

"Ouch!" I wailed. I could feel the new grafts rip from my cheek.

My mother bolted to me, "Oh no, Lesia! Let me look." She cradled my arm through hers and walked me inside as I wept in sorrow, embarrassment and pain. Sitting me in the kitchen, she peeled away the bandages and determined we needed to return to Miami right then to see Dr. Millard. It was Sunday; he would be there on Monday to "fix it."

My father, being the showman and always making everything a production spoke up, "Hey, I got a great idea: Let's move the party to the Safari. We can take the boat down the intercostal waterway to Miami (about a three-hour ride) and spend the night on the boat. We'll get a taxi to the doctor's office in the morning—all to support Lesia! Sound good everyone?" he bellowed.

Mother rolled her eyes again and to prevent an argument, surrendered. I lay on the back couch in the main salon as we motored to Miami. *Has he forgotten I get seasick? Doesn't he realize I'm injured and taking me to the doctors in a yacht full of drunk people is not in my best interest?*

Maybe he was trying to make the best of a bad situation. I didn't know. What I did know was that the next day meant surgery, IV's, drugs and pain—then more bandages, more stares from strangers.

My parents' marriage finally collapsed from the chaos. The empire came spiraling down. No surprise there. My mother and we three youngest moved to a smaller home, which we eventually lost. Beatrice went to live with a local family friend so we could visit. My grandparents moved to Arkansas, essentially going back to my grandmother's roots to die. My father lived on beautiful yachts with young women, wine and song, often dashing off to the Caribbean for libations and laughter. Yet he was always a simple heartbeat away from me; I continued to feel very connected to him. We were bonded in a soulful way.

One Saturday morning the phone rang.

"Hello?" I answered.

"Hi, Beaner." It was my father. "How's Daddy's little angel today?"

"I'm good, Dad, how are you?" I smiled underneath my tight scars.

"Awe, Baby, everyday above ground is a beautiful day. Do you have any plans this afternoon?" he asked.

"Well, I might go to the beach with my friend Cathy." I was unsure.

"Really? How about I meet you there?!" he replied. *Geez, something was up with him.* My father never went to the beach. He would go out in one of his boats with beautiful girls, champagne, shrimp, and, of course, a captain. Always on the water, rarely on the beach.

"You meet ME at the beach? Dad, you don't go to the beach!"

"Baby, where on the beach will you be, exactly? And at what time? Exactly! I need to know. This is important."

I was suspicious. He once purchased one of those bucket trucks that electric companies use to work on the high electric poles. He'd parked it along the beach, loaded with a cooler full of libations and a few partying girls. He then hoisted himself and the others high in the air in the bucket, so they could drink and watch the view. He claimed that he was the "highest" person in Fort Lauderdale. By the time of that phone call, he had sold that truck, but I was still wary.

I told him where we would be lying on the sand and what time.

"Promise me you will be there, Lesia!" he pleaded.

"I promise, Dad," I giggled. I had no idea what he was up to.

Hours later on the beach Cathy and I peeled off our bathing suit cover ups and greased up our legs in baby oil. I added a big floppy hat to hide my scars from beachgoers and the sun. I even forgot about the conversation with my father that very morning.

Suddenly, I heard a noise in the sky.

"Look, Cathy, a plane is writing in the sky with smoke … I'll bet it is a marriage proposal!" I squealed. "How cool is that!" I looked for a cuddly couple on the beach. No one was around. With that I remembered my dad saying he'd meet up with me. I hadn't mentioned it to Cathy and figured Dad had forgotten too. But the plane made me jump up to scour the street for a strange car. Nothing.

"Lesia!" Cathy cried. "Look! Oh my God! The plane … is writing a message for YOU … in smoke!!!"

My eyes moved to the sky, and I cocked my head to read: *Dear Beaner, I love you, DLS.* (Donald Lee Stockall). I sank in my beach chair, staring at my eccentric father high in the sky, feeling his love.

Some time later, my father announced: "Gloria, I want to take Darrin, Lesia and Cindy to the Caribbean for a year. I can teach them how to catch fish. They can snorkel every day off the back deck. Boating—it's the way of the islands."

"No, Don, they are in school," my mother replied.

"Oh, Gloria, will you loosen up?" he continued. "My children will learn more about life living on an island for a year than sitting in a stuffy classroom with the same boring people." As usual, his rationale was unconventional.

I leaned in to listen to the conversation through the wall of my safe room. I thought, no school for me for a year! I was giddy with excitement, yet dreaded the sun searing my scars. Ugh, I'd have to wear a big ugly hat and clothes to swim in. I sank back down in my bed.

"Don, you can't take them for a whole year, but I will allow them to go for the summer only." My mother was always willing to negotiate.

As we were packing to spend the summer in Providenciales, the phone rang. It was my father calling from the islands.

"Hi, Dad!" I squealed. Calls from the islands were rare and often from ship-to-shore radios.

"Hi, Baby, I'm looking so forward to you coming to see me," he sincerely shared.

"Me too, Dad, me too—can we swim?" I asked.

"Right off the back deck, Baby. The water is crystal clear; the sand is like white sugar. You will love it. I'm sitting here right now on the floating bar watching the fish swim in and out of the coral reef below me." And drinking a cocktail, no doubt, I thought.

"Well, Mom got me all packed. We're going to the airport in the morning. I miss you, Dad."

"I know, Baby, I miss you too and I'm ready for you, Darrin, and Cindy. We are going to have a lot of fun. We are also going to sail to Haiti while you are here." I had no clue where Haiti was, and didn't care. I was going to see my dad and nothing else mattered.

As I said goodbye and handed the phone to my mother I heard, "Lesia, wait! One more thing ... bring Beatrice," he said.

"Can we really, Dad! Beatrice can come to the islands with us?" I blurted.

"Sure, Baby, anything that will make you happy. See you tomorrow." I could picture him smiling into the phone.

My mother was not happy about Beatrice traveling with us. And it added a long list of preparations, cages, contacting the friend to see if we could take her, current shots and birth records, none of which we had. That created more chaos, something she thought she divorced months before.

The plane ride to the islands was in an old DC-3. Beatrice was supposed to be in a cage in the back of the plane, within reach. However, with our father the rule breaker as a role model, we couldn't bear the sight of Beatrice alone, terrified in the cage, chirping insensibly. After the plane took off, Cindy released her belt and crawled to the back of the very loud plane, where she unhooked the cage and grabbed Beatrice. Looking over his shoulder, the pilot squawked at us to leave the monkey in the cage. Cindy ignored him and held Beatrice on her lap.

The terrified monkey made not another peep. I was thrilled that Cindy had a special connection to Beatrice. That meant that when we were out together with the monkey, she attracted the attention, not me and my scars.

Island living was physically demanding in hot temperatures and full of dares. I learned to dive for conch, use an Hawaiian sling to spear grouper, and take small boats to isolated reefs to explore. I got to be with my dad every day. Wanting us to experience everything we could, my father decided we would take the boat and motor to Haiti, 10 hours away, in high seas.

We loaded the boat with island fruit and fishing gear, tied a dinghy to the stern, pulled anchor and headed southwest in the roughest seas. Any seafarer would've been afraid. We hit a massive storm. It was the first time I had seen my father scared. He had us tie ourselves to the decks so the waves and winds wouldn't blow us overboard. The best part was that we were isolated—no one stared at me.

After the summer was over, my mother picked us up from the airport in Fort Lauderdale.

"How was your trip?" She was really happy to see us, our return alleviating her deep-seated fear that Dad would try to keep us in the islands.

"Lesia, Sister George Margaret from St. Anthony's just called. Remember the catholic school we tried to get you in last year? Well, you have been accepted and will be starting sixth grade there in August, just three weeks!" My mother all but sang this news to me. She had total confidence that the nuns would take care of me, nourish my religious hunger, and protect me from teasing.

Did she know how I struggled internally?

My first thoughts were: *Crap, just when I was getting used to this public school and staying clear of my taunting classmates. I finally have a few friends to eat with at lunch. And, here we go again at a new school?*

My mom ramped up the school preparations for all three of us. Cindy was headed to a distant catholic high school; Darrin had permission to finish out his high school years in the public system. We shopped for school supplies and were measured for uniforms. My skirts had to touch the floor when kneeling and the ensemble included white socks and saddle shoes.

The stomachaches continued but this time it was different. I had my new coping skill, the mirroring technique already vetted in fifth grade. That seemed to work. If I kept pretending that I wasn't burned and made an effort to be nice to everyone, my new classmates would be nice to me.

Yeah, this was a lot for a twelve-year-old to handle. But hadn't I already handled the unimaginable pain of a burn injury? I was a master at survival. Yet, the shame of appearing damaged was additional. The normal teenager life—hanging out at crowded shopping malls, milling about school and doing anything to fit in—could be excruciating when you looked horrifically different.

My mom was right, though. Catholic school was better for my special situation. I found myself snuggled up with the energy of faith. God seemed everywhere. Crosses in every room, nuns floating through the halls with rosaries tied to their belt, hushed tones from their lips, and forced mass every Wednesday morning. I liked it. But for awhile, I remained leery of the nuns because I was still feeling the betrayal of Sister Catherine who in fourth grade had "made an example of me" in front of the class right after the accident. I continued to be guarded and protect myself, but I knew I had to make friends; I had to do this to survive. I needed to be like everyone else.

Don't get me wrong: The students at Catholic middle school were still children. Bullies and teasers were among them, but they didn't taunt me … because *nothing was wrong with me; I looked like everyone else.* This was my mantra.

The big distinction between public and catholic school was that catholic schools did everything possible to homogenize the students. It wasn't just the uniforms. There were no students like Elaine. No one had dirty torn clothes, broken shoes or adolescent hygiene issues. If a student was struggling with the simplest of needs, was hungry or missing a shoelace, the nuns swooped in and the problem was fixed, immediately.

One of my classmates was a boy named Matthew who had seizures. Each time a seizure occurred, students announced, "Sister Marie, Sister Marie! It's happening to Matthew." Sister Marie abruptly stood up and in a hushed yet firm tone told the class to help him lie on the floor, push away any desks, stand back, close our eyes and pray for Matthew. The nun always jumped in to put something in his mouth. Matthew convulsed on the floor, and seemed to go on forever. I was scared but I did watch Matthew's jolting body flail about.

As quickly as his shaking started, it would always stop. Matthew would open his eyes, look around in the stillness—our faces frozen in stares. A few students would step in and help him stand. I'd been in a hospital so many times, but I'd never seen anything like this.

Several whispers of "are you all right?" filled the room. Matthew invariably tried to hide the large pee stain on the front of his khaki pants. Sister appointed someone in charge of the room and she would escort Matthew to the school nurse's office.

When Sister Marie left the classroom, all was quiet—somber, no giggles, no teasing, no chalk flying through the air, just the feeling of compassion in the room. This behavior was important to me because I had facial reconstructive surgery coming up and was scared the kids would make fun of my bandaged face.

It seemed like a lesson in group dynamics. I felt grateful to my mother. Every penny she squeezed from my father for catholic school was worth it.

I spent another two years at St. Anthony's. As long as I began each day by acting as if I weren't burned, acting like every other girl in school, I was treated normally. I dared to let my silly self surface, cracked a few jokes I learned from my father, and made a few good friends. I began to feel safe—and maybe even a little cute in my powder blue uniform.

At the end of eighth grade, the annual list of "The Student Best Known For" came out. My name was at the end of the list. *Lesia Stockall: Best Personality.* My plan was working!

Entering high school at St. Thomas Aquinas was more of the same: as long as I acted normal, I was treated normally … usually. The added challenge, however, was the longing for romantic attention from boys. I had a few friends in school who were boys, but never any boyfriends. They were friends and friendly yes, but no, they were not interested in that way. Who would date a girl who had enormous scars on her face?

After two years traveling fifteen miles daily to attend St. Thomas, I convinced my mother to let me transfer to a high school closer to home. The caveat: it was a public school.

"Please, Mom, all the kids in our neighborhood go to public high school. My own brother goes to public school!" I pleaded ceaselessly. "St. Thomas is so far. I don't have any friends up here by our house because they all go to a different school—the one right down the street!" Like all teenage appeals, my cajoling was carefully deployed but unrelenting, to demonstrate a long-term commitment.

Mom resisted but at last surrendered, "Oh, all right, Lesia, but I think you are making a mistake. You won't learn as much and there are a lot of students."

My mother was right again. I left the safe haven of my small catholic school with crosses in every room, as well as nuns and teachers who cared. I traded the compassion in my fellow students' faces for being swallowed up in the mass number of students, prettier cliquish girls and boys who could care less that I existed.

My saving grace was two friends. Judy and Cathy attended the public school. Judy and I were friends since birth because our mothers were pregnant with us in Detroit. Our parents laughed and drank together, both heavily. Judy's mother, Carol, was like a second mom to me. And I'd known Cathy for some time. She had experienced my extroverted father skywriting directly above us on the beach and she was able to see beyond my scars into my heart, a heart I never felt safe enough to open to just anyone.

Prom was approaching. The school halls were a-buzz. Through Cathy's friends, I met a boy just before prom in my senior year. An attractive streetwise boy a year older than I, Joe was from upstate New York. Joe never graduated from high school; he came down to Fort Lauderdale for spring break and had a mysterious past. Wanting to fit in, I figured he would be a perfect date. While I worked the Joe angle, my mother scraped together money to purchase a beautiful pale blue dress for the prom. I had a lot invested in the *intention* of going, in wanting to appear normal.

Joe was a hard worker but he was trouble. I knew it; everyone knew it. But he was very cute and when an eighteen-year-old is terribly scarred, a cute boyfriend makes an important and validating accessory. Everyone seemed to accept Joe, except my father. Eventually my father had him run out of town. The blue dress remained in my closet, collecting dust. Another broken dream.

I knew I had to go forward, though. I finished school and handed my mother my diploma. Only my love and respect for her had kept me in school. It was her love that kept me from quitting, shrinking in a corner, drowning in self-pity.

Now what? I never wanted to return to a classroom again. I needed adventure.

Before long, I'd fallen in love with an Englishman. John was a funny, well skilled "bloke." My family adored him. To help John immigrate, I agreed to a secret short-term marriage. We were married by a friend of the court, just two days before we left to spend Christmas with his family and friends in England. The marriage was supposed to last only thirty days. Our plan was to get it annulled when we returned, after we cleared immigration.

However, John and I just kept traveling, all the while hiding our green-card marriage. Not for two years did we tell anyone we were married. Why bother? It would be annulled as soon as I found time to call my attorney. We both over-looked this. En route from Portugal to New Zealand, we stopped on Sanibel and Captiva Islands off the west coast of Florida. John's dream to coach tennis drove him to get a teaching job at a resort, anywhere beautiful. Dreams do come true.

John accepted a position as a teaching coach at South Seas Plantation, a sprawling, elite resort at the tip of Captiva Island. We cashed in our tickets to New Zealand, gave up backpacking to exotic places, and moved onto a houseboat for six months as part of his teaching contract. The six-month mark was approaching. I stood on the back of the house-boat, packing our backpacks for New Zealand. John came home for lunch. He told me they had offered him a year-round contract teaching at the resort.

I looked at him, glanced at the pelicans gliding over the glassy water and turned over my backpack and let my possessions fall to the deck. Captiva Island, not such a bad place to play tennis, fish, and chill.

The following year we bought a house on the island, a fishing boat and sporty vehicles, and even adopted a puppy, Wembley. Not long after, the marriage fell apart. The gorgeous islands were soon too small for a newly divorced couple. I was crushed but filled with a longing to find a deep purpose in life, the purpose my angels promised me years ago.

"Hey, Sis, why don't you come out here to California?" my older sister Chris suggested over the phone. We often step blindly into journeys of self-discovery. For me, my early twenties were one of those times. I had to grow spiritually, that meant leaving the safe womb of the island life. I moved to San Diego, determined to knock on doors of awakening … well, perhaps *bang* on doors.

Once in San Diego, I was grateful that Chris and her husband offered me the soft place to land in a new city where everyone was a stranger. But the launch pad was temporary; they had just welcomed my beautiful niece, Cassie, into the world so I had to hustle on out. I worked several jobs at once just to get by financially. I was a secretary for my brother-in-law's Vintage War Bird Company, sold clothing at upscale boutiques, and took care of scheduling court time and lessons at a small tennis club.

Meanwhile, I taught private lessons on any free court I could find. My car was a closet—several changes of clothes for the several different jobs in the same day. This hectic schedule was a far cry from my recent island life.

Money was hard to come by. While working, I managed to study and get a California real estate license. Hungry for change, any change, I called a local broker in the trendy area where I rented a small condo. That call would change my life in ways I never imagined.

We must be ready, trusting and open when we are pushed, pulled and finally hauled onto a path that can at first feel foreign but is finally and undeniably right.

Had I not been lucky to feel open, to trusting my path, I'd be in a place where darkness lives and struggles never cease.

"Yes! Actually I'm hiring sales agents," he told me on the phone. I scored an interview. Wearing my best suit and pearls, I walked out the door ready to score a job selling real estate. Who knew that I was walking into a massive tornado?

That I'd be picked up, whirled and deposited where my pain could fuel a passion that had nothing to do with real estate.

In my interview the broker asked a lot of questions, not so much about my real estate experience, but about my life in general. I thought this was a little odd. He tossed in an occasional real estate question but finished with, "I'd like for you to come back Tuesday for a second interview."

The following Tuesday, I showed up, looking professional and ready to work. The same odd dialogue in his office continued, but he remained sort of detached. Yet days later he called me back for another interview, saying he'd make up his mind then. There were four more interviews. I was running out of interview clothes let alone ways to "sell" myself. I thought, "What is going on here?" Yet I continued to go with the flow.

Finally, one night I received an unexpected phone call. The caller explained that she worked in the real estate office and was also the broker's roommate.

"Lesia, I have watched you come to your interviews over and over. You're always so full of hope and courage. Meanwhile, my roommate comes home every night and struggles with the way you look, your scars."

She continued, "I'm really sorry, Lesia. I didn't know if I should tell you or not, but he says that he can never hire you because of your scars. He doesn't know what to do, how to tell you this, and he is hoping you just get fed up and move on."

I sat down with tears welling up underneath my lids.

She continued, "He doesn't think that our clients will buy homes from you because of your burn scars. His strategy is to string you along so that you will quit coming in. If he finds out that I've called you, I'm going to lose my job and a place to live."

I couldn't believe what I was hearing.

"So, please don't tell him I phoned you. I'm sharing this with you because I admire your courage. You never gave up," she pleaded. "Go try another broker. Someone else will hire you, but he never will."

I hung up.

That moment was devastating—a critical life-changing point. *How was I to handle this? Where was I to go?* I was out of options, courage, and strength, and still looking scarred in a part of the country where superficial beauty was everything—running on empty.

I sat on the floor in my condo and wept. I could've been elated that I didn't need to come up with another dress for the interview, but I was devastated because this was my real world. It's not as if I had forgotten that people looked at me and treated me differently because I was physically scarred.

It had been more than a dozen years since the fire, and the hard work of forging ahead despite the discrimination came naturally to me by that point, like it does for a lot of people. It was as if I had decided, on some level, that the scars weren't there, that if I worked on being charming, knew how to have good conversations, and showed interest in people, my different appearance wouldn't matter.

I had convinced myself (sort of), that with enough clothes, hair product, pearls and good nature, the scars wouldn't be obvious. That roommate's call had been a huge awakening. That didn't mean, however, that I knew what to do about it.

"God," I whispered, "is this where I surrender? But surrender to what? Is this where I shift gears and do something else with my life?" *What if other people had scars on their faces and received that call? Would they jump off a cliff?* Instead of continuing to throw myself at my life pell-mell and as if I were Turbo Lesia, I stopped. I held still.

Trouble will come your way, but you need NOT give it a chair to sit on.

In that stillness, as scary as it was, I started to peek inside my heart and see my real pain. Yet when I examined my hurt with courage and faith, when I acknowledged the scarring that was (truthfully) a whole lot deeper than even the physical damage, I had an unforeseen reaction. I didn't feel anger. I didn't feel revulsion. I didn't feel self-pity.

You may think this sounds odd, as though I was denying my feelings but what I found was *comfort*—and beauty! What I felt was God and light, remembering my angels who visited me.

During the following days I began to see my scars as a part of me. Something I wore despite my denial. Others could see them and were affected. They couldn't help it and neither could I. I suddenly noticed that people treated me differently in public if I didn't have my makeup on to cover my scars.

I *suddenly* remembered the rejection, the dates I never got, the prom I never went to—all that rejection that I'd stuffed away, as if it didn't exist. It flooded back. However, I only allowed it to enter, but not sit with me for long.

For so many years when I saw my scars, I embraced them. Perhaps that was why other people did too—other people except Mr. "Broker," my greatest teacher.

I knew I was so much more than the scars I carried. I needed to find a path of renewal. I put myself in God's hands.

Not long after my "wake up call" I attended a small cocktail party where I was approached by a local plastic surgeon offering me what I considered a radical surgical procedure to "rid my face of scars." I called Dr. Millard, the surgeon in Miami who had performed all my reconstruction.

"Oh, Lesia, I'm not so sure about this," Dr. Millard shared over the phone. "Why don't you go see my colleague, Dr. Fisher, there in San Diego. He can tell you what is best."

I landed in the office of Dr. Fisher, not knowing he was the head of reconstructive surgery at the University of California, San Diego, Medical School. Sitting on the edge of Dr. Fisher's exam table, I fumbled through the explanation of the radical procedure offered to me.

I'd already logged lots of hours with reconstructive surgeons; I "wrote the book," from a patient's point of view. I was therefore astonished to see the look on Dr. Fisher's face. He was the head of a department of a very well regarded teaching hospital. Instead of looking clinical, he looked bewildered.

I blathered on.

"Wait a minute," he interrupted me. "We'll talk about your face in a minute. What is it you do for a living?"

"I work at a boutique at the Del Mar Plaza," I told him sheepishly, somewhat embarrassed because I *should* have been selling real estate.

"Retail? You work retail?" I nodded. He continued, "I'll get to my opinion on your procedure in a moment. First, I'm astonished at your recovery, Lesia. And I'm only partially talking about your scars here. I'm talking about your attitude and your energy level. In my opinion, you have much to offer. You really need to help children who are burned to recover. Become a role model."

I sat and stared. "You mean there are children who are burned?" I asked. This may sound crazy, but not since I left the burn ward in Detroit had I thought about other burn children. I had somehow encapsulated those anguished screams and completely wiped them from my memory.

"Lesia!" he smiled, "yes, there are other burn children in the world. I'm affiliated with the Burn Institute here in San Diego. Allow me to introduce you and perhaps you'll consider volunteering there.

CHAPTER FIVE

Burn Camp

*I wasn't prepared for the hunger
the children had for guided healing,
acceptance and self-love.*

Before I knew it, Dr. Fisher's introduction had me
hand-in-glove with the Burn Institute in San Diego. Even
though I was new to the burn foundation industry, they put
me in charge of recruiting volunteers to go with me to a burn
camp for a week. Most of the volunteers were firefighters.

My mind drifted. I didn't really know what I was doing, so
I winged it. (Interesting turn of a phrase considering how often
I relied on my angels.) The interviews were behind closed
doors. And so I began asking my inquiring questions to the
first unsuspecting firefighter.

"Why do you want to go to a burn camp for an entire week?" I asked.

"Because it sounds fun," the firefighter replied.

"Seriously, why do you really want to go to a burn camp?" I gently pried. Now I'm thinking, *if he shows me his heart, he's in.*

His voice lowered: "Well, I have a week off duty, and I like kids, so I thought why not?"

"Anything else?" I whispered back. I knew he was beginning to trust me.

"Well, yes. You know … being a firefighter I've had some really bad calls involving children." His voice drifted off. "In one incident a little boy was badly burned in a house fire, and I couldn't save him. We searched the house looking for him; he was hiding under the bed. And there were other calls … calls where children were severely injured in car accidents, I'd cut them out of the car, package them up, and the ambulance would dash them off to the hospital. I never really knew what happened to them. I'm looking for closure of some sort," he admitted.

> *Any activity in which we involve our whole heart has a dual healing—for us and the people around us. We need to look for it. Seek it out. There are people standing around in the simplest of situations whose souls can be fed by what we are doing or saying.*

"Thank you for your honesty," I smiled. "Of course you can accompany us to camp. We need you."

The entire time I was speaking to the firefighters in those early recruiting interviews, my thoughts returned to those who responded to my explosion thirty years prior. I had to listen to my gut as to who would be best, not only for the children we were chaperoning, but for myself, as well.

Just a few weeks later, I flew to northern California with four firefighters and eight burn-injured children for a week-long summer camp at Lake Shasta. Formally, I was a volunteer representative of the Burn Institute joining the staffing activities of another burn camp. The other burn foundation was directing the burn camp for fifty children from every part of the state. It was a long haul from the airport to the campsite deep into the mountains.

The anticipation of being around many burn-injured children gnawed at me. As we exited the van, meeting other camp volunteers was a whirlwind of hectic emotion.

Being with others who had severe burn injuries—others who were children—for the first time nearly sent me running back for a sixth interview with the real estate broker. I was overwhelmed with excitement, pain, love, and confusion. On the other hand, I felt I had finally arrived "home." An inner voice told me just to keep moving forward, answering my hunger to heal. But heal from what? I asked myself.

Fire had robbed me of my childhood, which was where these children were, and from my experience I knew that they too would have additional trials. Emotion bubbled within me. I needed to bear down and love myself through it all. This was going to be a long week.

Everywhere I looked that week, I saw myself. Fifty children meant fifty of my own broken hearts running around stuffing, masking, and drowning the physical, emotional and psychological pain. Suffering a traumatic burn injury delivers the whole whammy, plus the apprehension of never again feeling safe.

These children needed ways to somehow deal with the coming challenges … as did I! And I needed to hit the mother lode of strength and courage—plus inspiration.

It was day two at burn camp. The program director was holding a session for the girls in a dusty, dirty facility room. She instructed the children to hold up a mirror to themselves, look into the mirror, straight into their eyes and repeat to themselves: "I love and accept you just as you look." Horrified by the cluelessness of this approach, I wanted to bolt and never return.

Instead, I stepped gently out the door. A nurse was sitting on a wooden bench under a tree, reading. I made it to the bench, put my head into my hands and wept. My tears held every piece of the explosion and outrage I felt within. I stayed on that bench nearly through the night, crying, as the nurse held me. My tears competed with Niagara Falls in velocity and volume.

The remainder of the week I seesawed between intense emotions, listening to the horrific stories, and enjoying playtime with the girls. Playing with the cute firefighters was a gift as well.

One little girl, whose parents had *deliberately* burned her, stole my heart. Late one night in our cabin, she whispered to me, "I begged the judge please not to send me back to live with my mother, because she hurts me with her curling iron, see?" With that she pulled up her pajama top to show me burn marks on her chest in the shape of a curling iron.

"So where did you go live then?" I asked.

"I went to live with my father, but then he did this …." She again pulled up her pajama top to show me another scar—the shape of a triangle. He had burned her with an iron. "So I'm back with my mother now. I hope she doesn't burn me anymore. It hurts!" She began to weep.

At this moment I felt blessed that my burn injury was a result of an accident. My family loved and cared for me and would never abuse me like this poor little girl standing before me. Who knew just because we smelled gas that our house would blow up? This blew our lives into tiny shards of glass. And those shards didn't stop cutting.

Each time someone stared at me, another cut into my soul. This little girl had her own parents' name embedded in each shard.

With this encounter, I began to understand the "intention" behind our pain, clearly. A severe trauma had left both this little girl and me disfigured. For me, it had taken and was still taking an enormous amount of energy, strength, and determination to get through the treatments and healing phase. And the healing was both physical and mental.

When the injury includes the loss of a family member or is the result of abuse, it makes additional demands on emotions. While overcoming the physical pain, the injured must also grapple with grief, forgiveness, and/or loss of trust. Often times that pain is far worse than any tub room experience of nurses using wire brushes gnawing over dead burned skin to prevent infection.

Whether pain is physical, mental, or emotional, its intention is a direct reflection of the level of healing we seek.

In many ways, this little girl's challenges were greater than mine, and I really longed to help her.

The cabins were "rustic." Ours had four sets of bunk beds with plastic wrapped mattresses on rusted springs. I had the younger children assigned to me. At night I lay awake listening to their whimpering, a heartbreaking and familiar murmur of pain mixed with terror and loneliness. Their every movement made the rusted bedsprings creak. It was as if I had been transported right back to the burn ward, those twenty years ago.

I honestly didn't know how I was to perform as the "adult" to these children the next day, caring for them when my wounded self cracked open wider as I peeked at each scar on the precious little bodies around me. I was becoming raw, open, and present.

How did I get here? The setting was like being in a pool of anguish in the middle of the forest. Was I ready for this intensity? My injury happened in the late sixties, when people still processed their survival silently—I had coped by being alone with my grief. For years I had desperately tried to look and feel normal.

I had never seen a therapist after the explosion. I couldn't run from my intense pain of being burned when it was staring right back at me in the faces of children now around me. I wanted to bolt, to escape. But to where? Lying on that creaky mattress, I had "hit a wall."

For some reason, it was time to stop running and pretending and to face the truth about how I looked and felt. I needed to heal this pain and ultimately accept me. But what did this really mean? I was learning that the crack in awareness that pain pierces comes in many disguises. The explosion left me with scars, but more unsettling, it taught me not to trust life—that at any moment a house could blow up, people could die.

Picking my head up off the pillow and struggling to focus in the shadows lit by moonlight, I became aware that, hard as I had worked to create jobs and a career, perhaps my path was already chosen and it was a different path.

Remembering the angels who had visited me first in the basement, then in the hospital bed, I thought, "Are they here now?" I wept myself to sleep.

The days at camp were injected with laughter followed by silent tears. I made it through the week, gaining strength, disappearing into the woods for brief connections with prayer. I needed a reminder of God and the angels who had promised not to abandon me. By day four I was getting into the groove and beginning to feel at home.

I found a glittery wire in the arts and crafts room and constructed a halo and then pinned it to my head where it remained throughout the week. I'd do anything to call my angels just like the people who wear tinfoil to attract aliens. I was desperate.

I wasn't the only one there that was nervous and frozen with insecurities.

Jeff, a firefighter from San Diego who had flown up with me, was overseeing five boys, ages six through eight. One night at dusk, Jeff appeared with a terrified look on his face.

"Lesia, there you are!" Jeff was panting. "I have failed you. You need to send me home."

"What?!" I exclaimed. "Why? What happened?"

"It's Nathan, I've lost him!" Jeff blurted out.

"What? Where? How?" Now I too was alarmed. "When did you last see him?"

"He had to go to the bathroom. I pointed to the restrooms, just through the trees, and then I looked away to answer another question." Poor Jeff.

There were thousands of questions from these boys who were clearly awestruck to have a real live firefighter at their beck and call, but Jeff wasn't a parent and wanted to please all of them—all at once. It was easy to get distracted. "And damn if he didn't just disappear!" he panted, then finished with, "George is watching my other four boys so I can look for Nathan!"

"OK, Jeff, calm down, we'll find him."

"Lesia, I'm so sorry. You need to send me home. I'm not a good fit for this. I don't know how to be a counselor. Oh, I can't believe I lost a child!" Jeff was a wreck.

"Jeff, I chose you because I know you have what it takes to help these boys. You're not going home; the boys need you and I need you."

"Well, apparently one boy didn't need me!" Jeff cried.

The camp facility was isolated, yet there were more than eighty of us counselors and children mucking about. Nathan had to be somewhere.

As I was talking Jeff off his self-defeating cliff, I looked up to see Nathan standing innocently in the doorway of the cafeteria. He had soiled his pants and was buried deep in an ice cream cone.

"There he is!" I shouted.

Jeff snapped his head around and dashed toward Nathan.

"Where have you been?" Jeff cried.

"Right here eating ice cream. Want some?" Nathan offered up his sticky, dripping mess of a cone.

"I thought you were going to the bathroom?"

"Well, I was, but then I saw the ice cream being served," Nathan mumbled in between licks.

"Buddy, I was so worried about you!" Jeff looked down at his soaked, soiled pants, put his arm around Nathan and whispered, "Come with me, little buddy, we'll get you changed. And tomorrow we're going fishing."

Jeff continued as a camp counselor with me for years.

After the week at burn camp was over, I returned with the vision of starting my own burn camp. The pain and sometimes dissatisfaction of the mountain camp was cathartic. But given my intimate knowledge of the path burn-injured children shared, I felt I had something powerful to offer. Moreover, it was plainly too awful to watch well-intentioned adults adding to the kids' misery—not mitigating it.

Channeling my dad's entrepreneurial nature and my mother's steady strength, I just knew I could pull off a better program, and felt sure I could recruit firefighters and find a location too.

"I can do this," I pleaded with the executive director where I had been a volunteer for just a month.

The executive director gave me the go ahead to start a camp in San Diego under his watchful eye. I was on a mission not only to heal those around me but to heal myself as well. I found a local camp facility to rent for one week every summer. Moving forward with my vision, I recruited trusted volunteers, and then sought out boys and girls with serious burns from all over the state and beyond.

Throughout, I felt like one beggar telling another beggar where the bread was.

My devoted volunteers were mostly firefighters like Jeff who were there for me, for the children, and for themselves. Men and women from regional fire departments agreed to design and run different areas of the camp program—the roller-hockey, the challenging ropes course, basketball, swimming, arts and crafts, campfires—all typical camp activities.

I spiced up each camp week. There were visits from medic helicopters, foam machines delivered from wildland fire departments to pump foam for us to play in on the large grassy field, archery and live stage plays such as *Beauty and the Beast.* How appropriate!

The process had its own learning curve. There were hiccups in the beginning. Counselors sneaking on the ropes course at night landed one of them a helicopter ride to the hospital for a broken pelvis. The first hour of the first camp I caught a teenage boy in the shower stall smoking pot. There was the homesickness, the camp romance gone sour, and the fire department photographer I kicked out for bad language. But I wasn't giving up. I tightened up the reins and developed my own leadership style in subsequent camp sessions. We set strict rules in place and we were on our way to success.

Burn camp became the Burn Institute's flagship. Not having access to patients to support throughout the year, I spent my time after camp participating in fundraisers, sharing my story with various groups to seek funding, recruiting, and ultimately planning for the next camp. I felt unstoppable. This was my passion, which I pursued while juggling two other part-time jobs and college.

My continuous search for what is real in life continued. Opportunities to meet real people with hearts of strength and love kept presenting themselves to me—or trying to. One of my gigs was in retail, working in a lofty designer boutique in Del Mar. This was a third job I was holding down while going to college and working for the Burn Institute. Early one evening a handsome man sauntered in seeking a gift for his girlfriend.

"May I help you?" I approached him casually.

"I'm looking for something for my woman," he replied is a seductive tone while twirling the keys to his Bentley around his finger.

In trying to narrow down his choices, I began to ask questions clarifying what type of gift he was looking for.

"Oh, something sexy to wear because she is absolutely beautiful ..." he said as he blew a kiss into the sky.

Staying on point I continued, "What size is she?" Usually men don't know their woman's size. "Is she bigger or smaller than me," I dared. This measure usually works in helping men shop, but not that day. With that, he looked me up and down, slowly.

"No, no, no ... not like you ... she is *beautiful* ... she's got the perfect body!" Using his accent to accentuate.

I couldn't help myself. Something within me snapped.

"Excuse me, do you really know what beauty is ... clearly not!" I inched closer to him, to lock his eyes while I continued my rant. "You tell me she is beautiful. So when you wake in the middle of the night worried over your latest business meeting, does she whine because you woke her ...? Or does she sit up, rub your back and ask you how she can help? Will she still be there when God forbid you lose your wealth? As you watch her walk across the room, can you visualize her caring for you when you are broken? That's beauty!"

I continued, "Will she be there to comfort you at the death of a loved one? Will she care for you when you are ill with the flu, or worse, cancer? Does her beauty run deep into her heart so you see her light first as she enters a room and not her large plastic boobs?"

He stared at me as if I was dangerous, but it didn't stop me. I was on a roll. "Will she care for your animals while you are away, or your aging parents; will she hold you when you are afraid ... Mister, *that is beauty.*"

Finally, I stopped.

There was silence for what seemed several minutes.

"Thank you," he whispered. "I don't think I will be buying any gifts for her."

He turned around and walked out.

I had blown a good sale, and if he knew the owner, my job was gone too.

A few days later I received a beautiful bouquet of roses and an invitation to dinner. I declined the dinner and kept the roses.

In a few short years my group at the Burn Institute became a well-oiled machine, a tight team of volunteers with more than eighty children at every camp. Our reputation grew. Volunteers poured in seeking to be a part of my team. I was proud of my crew of volunteers and their cemented devotion. Even fire battalion chiefs laid down their gold badge and rank to work the entire week next to their first year fire-fighters who scrubbed burn garments for the children during burn camp, cut up meat at dinner for children who had lost fingers or hands and dried kids tears from knees scraped on the ball field.

Like other volunteers, firefighters exhibited comfort, compassion, and consistent caring toward the overall program. They understood trauma and burns, and desperately needed a touch of healing in their own hearts. They were tremendously nurturing, which reinforced the wisdom of my improvised interview style to which each man and woman had been subjected.

Behind closed doors my prospective volunteers, who were professional firefighters, watched a video of burn camp and listened to the children's stories. Many of them wept. I once asked an applicant why he had become a firefighter. After a long hesitation, obviously struggling with emotions, he quietly spoke.

Wounds occur throughout our journey on Earth, as does healing. We never really know the depth of pain that experiences bring, not in ourselves, not in others, especially not in those who appear so brave.

"When I was a little boy, our house burned down. I stood on the curb and watched the fireman carry my mother's body out on a stretcher." He started to cry. "I knew that day that I wanted to do what I could to never let that happen to anyone else, ever." As it turned out, his heart was too heavy to volunteer the entire week of camp, however, he did volunteer one day with an activity.

The bond between the firefighters and the children at camp was special. Firefighters don't often hear the outcome of the patient they treated on the street, at the car accident or house fire, so this venue was a way for them to follow through. Every session was its own unending miracle. Hearts breaking open.

I rose before dawn to prepare for the day. I cradled some coffee and ventured out to the porch. I found a firefighter volunteer sitting in a deck chair, weeping.

"Joe, is everything OK?" I whispered.

"Lesia, my heart is breaking for these children, what they have been through … I feel so helpless here. I want so badly to fix them, give them a better life." Joe buried his face in his hands.

"Joe, we *are* fixing them. We are loving them. You are demonstrating to the children that people do care, that we care," I shared.

"Lesia, what happened to these children could have been avoided. I'm so angry and saddened that most of these children are burned from neglect."

I'd seen tears from firefighters at burn camp before … and not because they broke their finger playing roller-hockey. An open heart from first responders crowns them with grace, a gift wasted on no one.

Watching the children arrive at camp always delivers miracle moments if your eyes are open. One of our volunteers arrived at camp. She was an older woman who had been burned in a car accident. Eloise had lost the fingers on her hand in the fire and was left with only a palm. As we were helping with her luggage, a young boy named Damian walked up the path.

We knew he had been wounded severely by playing with matches; his mattress had caught fire and then his body. He too was left with a "paw." Timidly, he stopped and stared at Eloise's paw. She held her hand in the air.

"Hey, have you ever seen a paw like this?" Eloise smiled.

Damian held up his own paw as if to introduce it to hers. Damian then tore away, running to catch up with the other boys. It was day one and we were already trying to cover our tears.

Towards the end of camp I saw Joe handing his firefighter's badge to a little girl.

"I know you are having surgery next week," he said to her.

"Yeah, I'm really scared," she whimpered.

"Do you know what this represents?" Joe asked her as he pulled his badge out of his bag. "This badge represents courage and bravery."

She never looked up, frozen in fear of the looming pain that accompanies yet another surgery.

"I want you to have this badge. Keep it until after your surgery. You deserve to have all the courage and bravery this badge represents."

I pulled Joe aside.

"Joe, you can't give her your badge. You're on duty tomorrow. Your captain will call you out!" I cried.

"Lesia, if my captain asks where my badge is, I'm going to tell him that he must ask that little girl over there for it."

These miracles happened all the time—all the time if one watched for them.

Once the children went home, I received letters from the parents or the children themselves thanking me for the experience. On the surface, it was just camp. We played games. Yet seeing other children with scars strengthened each child. I felt, however, that they needed more support.

So I added a support session into the week at burn camp. I divided the children into groups and let them share their story of how they were burned. Treading in uncharted waters and with no licensed therapist, I asked myself what harm could come from the children telling their story to an attentive audience? It worked.

Yet I wasn't prepared for, yet suspected, the emotion and hunger the children had for guided healing, acceptance, and self-love. The need for this type of release outlet was blatantly apparent to me, so I added a second support session during the week. But these children needed professional help, more than what we were improvising. It was beautiful to watch, their eyes trusting their path, yet fearful all in the same breath.

But it was a shame not to continuously address the abundance of pain and uncertainty in the children, especially when we had them away from their often-toxic lives.

After the first camp I approached my boss at the Burn Institute.

"I think we need to design a new program within the camp week to increase the emotional support for the children.

Maybe hire a therapist to inject a component into the program about their burn injury."

"No, Lesia. It's just camp. Kids want to have fun," he replied.

"Well, while that's true, we're still missing an opportunity to help the children further, on a deeper level. Let's expand the program while they are all in our presence," I pleaded.

He still rejected my idea. In listening to my gut I felt it was because an additional component of the camp would cost the Burn Institute money. Deeper healing couldn't happen with just volunteers alone. We would need to pay for a licensed therapist or two but the executive director wanted to hire more fundraising staff.

Even so, as the camps went on over the years at my direction, I never lost my desire to help the children heal—and the need continued to present itself to me.

My assistant during camp was a San Diego firefighter named Dave. When I met Dave and his wife at a party, I immediately had a "feeling." Though not everyone admits to it, most of us know when we make a new acquaintance whether that person will walk our path, see our light, and fulfill a duty as part of God's plan. My intuitiveness rarely lets me down.

We attract to our lives what we feel

Dave had exactly what I needed in directing camp and steadying my passion. After we began working together, Dave's honesty, compassion, and leadership pushed burn camp forward—all with my vision at heart.

The real champions in our lives are not only the ones who constantly make us feel good, lift us up, congratulate us. They are also those who push us, show us a mirror, remind us when we are running away, stop us from stuffing what needs to be acknowledged, all with love.

Dave saw what I didn't see, and backed me up in times of struggle. He became a vehicle for my work, cradled my concerns, and held the flag for what I believed to be true. He helped me establish a well-connected team.

I deeply loved the children at camp who now totaled more than eighty each summer. I continued to see a piece of myself in each of them. I felt peace in my heart as a director in creating this camp ... until the day when a few passing teenage girls changed my life forever.

It was midweek at burn camp. The late afternoon sun cast our shadows on the grass. With my heart full, I felt content to cradle what God wanted me to do—gather burn-injured children and help guide them on their path.

God speaks to us all the time. If we sit quietly, with openness to what we need to hear, we know what to do next. Only our fear of stepping forward holds us back. To listen is to live.

Dave and I, standing on a grassy hill, saw three teenage girls returning from a session. Their heads were downturned and they looked very sad.

Noticing this all too familiar posture, something struck me. "My God, Dave, I'm failing," I whispered. Our program had a severe shortfall. I couldn't ignore it anymore.

"Failing?" he sputtered. "What? Lesia, look at what you created here. This environment is beautiful, a safe place for the children to play without other people staring! How can you say you are failing?"

"Dave ..." my thoughts slowly forming into words, "camp wraps up in two days. What's going to happen to those teenage girls come Monday when the camp is over and we are finished spoiling them with all this attention and fun?" I continued, "They will return to face rejection, staring, teasing, going on errands where small children point and say hurtful things. Return to school where they will never get asked to school dances ..."

Dave stood silently next to me, listening. In retrospect, I can say that Dave was often standing close to me when I sensed a transition about to happen; he guarded my soul without either one of us really knowing it. His presence assured a sense of safety and dedication, bigger than the both of us. Although we have tried. We could never explain the connection but it was there, strong as steel, delicate as silk.

I trusted that something big was going to happen, but didn't pay attention to the risk that invariably comes with change.

"Who will teach them to deal with the rejection from boys, with not going to prom or with how to cope with their family's reaction to them? How will they know how to apply corrective makeup? Or that there is even makeup out there to minimize their scars? Who will teach them how to handle staring and teasing? No one!" I continued. "They have no place to go."

My own memories came flooding back. "How will they survive that, Dave? I'm not *teaching* them anything here. I'm letting them play roller hockey and swim. Ultimately, this doesn't really do them any good."

I began to zero in on this obvious truth. *I'm doing them a disservice, my inner voice rumbled. I'm showing them what their life could really be like if they looked normal.* But they don't.

Dave sometimes knew me better than I knew myself. At times I caught him watching me. Sometimes he caught me watching him. We both knew when a push was needed and each was eager to be the one to push the other.

This time, he grinned. "Well, Lesia, what are you going to do about it?"

"I don't know, but I'm going to do something. Watch me." Just like I knew he would.

At that moment, three younger girls, Monica, Jennifer and Yaderia, all age six, ran up to me in their little Tweety Bird bathing suits with flip-flops on their feet, cartoon beach towels under their arms. "Miss Lesia, can you come play in the pool with us now, pleeeease?" As I looked down at their terribly scarred faces, I saw the faces of angels.

"Oh, girls, I'm so sorry ... I need to meet with a few volunteers first ... but look at your faces. You all look like little angel faces!" It just popped out of my mouth. The vision, my future, came over me like a freight train. (This moment brought such an epiphany that I still keep the photo of these girls nearby eighteen years later.)

"Now, run along," I continued, "and take my heart with you to the pool. I will try to get there soon, OK?" As they ran down the grassy hill to the pool I shouted after them, "Make sure you have a counselor with you and wear your floaties!"

I loved those little girls as though they were my blood. It was as though my heart were running outside my body.

The last two days of camp, I felt a flicker of light coming alive in my soul. I knew then my path had already changed. As I lay in bed that evening trying to piece together what had happened, visions of my future muddled with the next day's schedule of activities. Dave peeked through my cracked door, hoping to switch out his radio battery.

Bonding happens when the heart is open to love and healing amidst such pain, any pain. To prevent us from drowning in pain—we must KEEP our heart open and allow love to keep us floating forward. It is the only path that heals.

I looked up somewhat startled as he stood in the doorway. "Oh yeah, you have that look in your eye, Lesia. You're onto something," he mumbled.

OK. I was busted. "I'm thinking of the faces of the little girls heading to the pool. They really looked like faces of angels to me, Dave. Did you see them too?"

Dave smiled. He was already scared of my visions, so I let him off the hook by focusing on task at hand. "There's your charged battery, Mr. Catalyst," I said, pointing to the radio chargers across the room. We often had witty names for each other. And he was clearly a catalyst for me, creating a safe place for me to dream. I never knew what I was to him, although I suspected.

"Good night, Dave," I whispered. "Good night, Director," he replied. He closed the door. I lay back and prayed for one more day at camp with no injuries.

Closing this particular camp down was different than past years, not the usual angst that went with watching the kids don their social armor before they loaded onto the bus to return to their difficult reality. Something had changed. I felt an excitement for my path and a path I could introduce to others.

CHAPTER SIX

Back Into the Fire

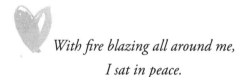

With fire blazing all around me,
I sat in peace.

I'm no sissy, but I do have a few phobias. There's the healthy fear of sharks. Add to that my dread of putting gas in my car. I'd always relied on visitors to light my fireplace. When someone lit a BBQ, I quietly slipped into the house far away from a potential blast.

And above all, I wouldn't live in a house or apartment with natural gas. Period. I liked to think, though, that I was a brave person and that I wouldn't run from fear. Why then did my boyfriend at the time, Allen, keep telling me that fear was my greatest teacher?

In addition to my own hang-ups, I witnessed fear every day at burn camp. The faces of the burned children reflected my insecurities. The San Diego Urban Search and Rescue Team rigged up a rope course at burn camp for the children. My job was to stand at the bottom encouraging the children to climb up to the high platform and walk across this plank.

"Joey, trust yourself! Look forward, don't look down ... find your center!" I shouted.

Joey would tremble with fear, putting one foot in front of the other, slowly.

"Face your fear. It's only fear," I continued. Yeah, right.

The children's fearful expressions reminded me that my explosion still had its demons. How could I help them to have courage and trust in themselves if I was terrified of fire? Fear was in me, coursing through my blood and I needed to get over it.

Privately (never out loud), I wondered what would happen if I could go back into a raging fire. If I faced fire with the courage of an adult, not the scared little girl I was, would I be free of that fear forever? *Be careful what you ask for—it will find you,* I warned myself.

As a representative of the burn foundation, I attended a fire fighting training conference in 1994 with a colleague. We checked into the hotel, registered our booth, grabbed our brochures and meandered by the welcoming cocktail reception in the hotel lobby. Muscling through the loud firefighters felt like a large family reunion where I knew no one, I belonged.

We found two stools at the packed bar and ordered a drink. We nearly had to shout to be heard over the boisterous laughter of hundreds of firefighters celebrating their reunion.

Across the room a man stood out among the others. With slightly grey hair and bellowing laughter, he seemed to be holding court. Without thinking I abruptly popped off my chair and made my way to him. It was as though I had been pushed. Little did I know my life was about to change forever.

"You are the loudest and most obnoxious man in this place. With hundreds of firefighters here, all I can hear is you," I bravely shouted to him. "Why do you need to be so loud?"

"Nice to meet you too, er um … your name, please?" he stumbled.

"Lesia, my name is Lesia!" Suddenly I regretted my approach and giving him my real name.

"Well, Lesia, I'm just a gentle puppy dog. Look!" With that he grabbed a strapping man next to him and proceeded to lick his face. "See, I'm just a gentle kind of guy."

Appalled, I strutted back to my seat. Eventually, though, he came inching over to where we were sitting. Did someone pop him off his stool to come see me as well?

As time marched on, the lobby cleared out and I found myself sitting at a table with him, alone. He was a captain for the San Diego Fire Rescue Department. "So, how were you burned?" he asked. I thought, *wow, pretty ballsy for a guy I just met.*

Other firemen always avoided the question—perhaps acknowledging that something went wrong under their watch and a burn-injury represented failure. Or maybe circumspection—their own fear of how dangerous firefighting can be.

I described the tragedy. He tilted his head with focus as though he were on the fire ground at a scene, investigating the finite ash to seek its origin. The more he listened, the more I opened up about the accident. He postulated, from his extensive knowledge of fire behavior, what had probably happened, the consistency of the natural gas and why it exploded when it did. I was in awe.

He said that given that natural gas in my grandparents' home had been leaking for three days, every time my grandmother opened the window the ratio of gas to oxygen changed. This lowered the ignition point. When the ratio reached the perfect match for an explosion, the gas found an ignition source—the pilot light on the hot water tank. And my little nine-year-old self was standing two feet away in the basement.

The fire captain and I sat through moments of silence as I absorbed this new knowledge. It had been twenty-four years since the accident and until then no one had explained to me why the house exploded. My family was in too much pain and I was consumed with healing my burns. This stranger with eyes as blue as jewels made sense of an event

I had only ever associated with screams and burning flesh, all my own.

The catastrophic event had technical causes. I was pretty intrigued by his interest and insight into what had happened.

Then it shot out of my mouth—straight from my heart: "I would really like to face my fears of fire and get over that fear." *Holy smokes. Did that really come out of my mouth?* My mind was detached from what I was really saying.

"I can do that for you, Lesia," he sputtered.

I wasn't expecting that kind of an answer.

"Oh no, wait, really, really. I need to think about this ..." I heard myself stammer.

"I train firefighters at the academy and can set up a controlled burn, put you in our yellow turnout firefighting gear, and teach you how to hold a hose. And then I'll take you back into the fire," he offered casually, as if it were a cakewalk.

What was I doing here? What was this stranger offering me?

The captain continued, "I'll teach you how to put out the fire—so you won't be afraid anymore. In three months my team and I are burning down houses at the marine base in Twenty Nine Palms just two hours from San Diego. If you want to come out, I'll put you through the fire."

In saving face and gathering my thoughts, I replied off-handedly, "Oh, that sounds interesting. I'll check my calendar."

We said our goodbyes. As I headed to my hotel room, I planned two trajectories—one was my escape from this crazy idea, and the other was the remote possibility of accepting the captain's offer to free myself from my over-whelming terror of fire.

I continued to ponder. *I have three months to wiggle out of this,* I rationalized. I can pray, meditate, and snuggle with God and see what answers surface. I can call a therapist and ask her if I'm nuts to try this. *Is this really what I want to do?* I can conjure up all sorts of excuses in three months, or not.

But how awesome would it be to be free of the fear of fire and see the angels who rescued me many years ago! My newfound fire captain would never understand the angel component. That I would have to keep from him. Yet I didn't have any doubts about the angels. None whatsoever.

In the safety of my hotel room, I washed the makeup off my marbled, scarred face. Peering into the mirror, I saw both a frightened little girl and a woman who had the courage to do whatever it took to be free. I gathered these integrated energies together, crawled into bed, and continued to struggle with my recently presented opportunity.

Pouring rain awakened me the next morning. I made a dash for the convention center, holding my conference book over my head. The exhibit hall was enormous—a massive room full of fire trucks, rescue exhibits and thousands of firefighters, trainers, sales people, and vendors, all in the business of saving lives.

As I meandered in the rows of gadgets and rescue equipment, I heard his voice.

"Hey there … Lesia, right?"

It was the fire captain. "Glad I ran into you. I just secured a new contract with the sheriff's department in Poway, California, and I'm holding a controlled burn in three weeks. Are you game?" So much for my three months of equivocation, I thought. And good grief—Poway was only ten miles from my home. Now I had fewer excuses.

Before I could answer, he leaned over me and shook a colleague's hand. It was a salesman with the Scott Firefighting Equipment exhibit booth. Scott is a leader in the industry for breathing apparatus. Their exhibit was quite impressive.

"Hey there, Joe. How are ya?" Before Joe could answer, my newfound fire captain launched into my story, sharing with Joe that I was thinking of going into a "burn down" with him to face my fears … and did he have a mask I could try on?

He's pulled me so far into this adventure, I thought. I was speechless.

Joe from Scott Firefighting was intrigued. "Oh really? Well, that's pretty courageous," he commented as he fleetingly looked over my facial scars. "I'll tell you what …" he said, handing my friend the fire captain a very high tech, expensive mask off his display table, "She can use this. When you're finished, just bring it back."

Damn. Suddenly I was everyone's business? I was already in deep enough that it was as though I had no say—just a tremendous feeling of trust in this captain. *What am I doing? How do I stop this runaway train?*

As I stood in the middle of the exhibit floor with people nudging to maneuver around us, Joe and the captain fitted the mask onto me. *What the hell is going on here?*

"Yes, it fits. Here take this mask home, Lesia. Wear it in front of the TV or reading and get familiar to the claustrophobic sensation," the captain ordered.

How in the hell does he know I'm claustrophobic?

The conference came to a close and I flew home haunted by thoughts of going back into the fire. I only had three weeks to get out of this, or face it.

Allen, my boyfriend, was a beautiful, funny, very spiritual man who daily taught me about the power we possess and how to trust the light within ourselves. He was very new agey—radically different from the grounded, bellowing fireman I had just met. Allen was my best teacher about life on so many levels. Seeing more in me than I ever had, he encouraged me to go to massage school and honor the gift I had for healing.

Not only were we intense lover-mates; we were playmates, and mates in daily precious moments. And Allen taught me how to boogie board. We were crazy about life and each other. Each morning as the sun came up we'd ponder either to make love or boogie board. Both got equal attention.

We would peel out of bed, grab our boards and fins, and head to the waves. If we didn't make the morning ocean swim, we'd go at sunset. Dusk in the waves always brought my fear of sharks. As the sun sank into the water, I'd start worrying,

"But what about sharks? Let's go. It's getting dark," I'd yip to him from another wave.

"Just one more ride," he'd shout back. "Be the master of your fear, Lesia!"

Allen taught me how to peel the layers of pain away from within my heart and gather courage to face whatever surfaced through visualization and meditation, as I had done as a child to find safety.

Little did we know that our two years together was preparing me for a life-changing experience. In our time together, meditation enhanced my faith, allowing God's light to consume the darkness where I kept my lingering fear.

Allen picked me up curbside at the airport. "How was your trip to the fire conference?"

I described the conference and the interesting things I learned. I could hardly remain calm when I told him that I'd been offered an opportunity to go back into a fire, to face my fears.

"Wow, that sounds interesting," Allen hesitated. He must've seen the excitement in my eyes. "When are you doing this? And who is this fireman who is taking you into a burning structure?" I could hear the apprehension in his voice.

Yet my journey was well under way and the day was fast approaching. Nothing Allen could say would stop me. He knew it too.

During the nights before the burn down, I lay in bed listening to whatever angelic music I could get my hands on. I reached to drift into meditation, to find soft moments to ponder if I really wanted this. In the meantime, the fire captain called.

"Come to the station. You can try on turnouts (yellow fire gear) to see if they fit." He continued, "I have two female firefighters on my crew. I'm guessing their uniforms might work." All I could think was, "he's totally buffaloing me." Meanwhile I focused on spiritual enlightenment, the feeling I'd had when my angels rescued me from the basement thirty years before—guiding me out the hole with their white light. Hopefully, I thought, I'll see them again.

I couldn't share my yearning to see angels again, not to a fire captain who bellows and moves with bravado. I felt no connection, except profound trust. Where did this over-whelming sense of trust come from?

As I pulled up to his fire station to try on the gear, its large doors opened and out rushed the engine, its siren blasting, to an emergency. With fear swirling in my head, I concluded, "This is a sign. I'm not supposed to go back into the fire."

I drove back to my office. The captain called two hours later.

"Sorry, we got a call. I saw you pull up but we had an emergency." He continued, "I'm back on duty in two days; we can try again."

Again? Yeah right. "Oh, sure," I gently responded, but two days later the same thing happened; I arrived at the station just as the engine was pulling out, sirens blaring. *Was I crazy to go back and into a burning building?* I spent days praying, thinking, and obsessing, but it became clear: *I'm doing it!* I trusted this fire captain more than I trusted myself at that point.

A week later, it worked. I arrived at the fire station and the crew was there, standing with the captain. The captain helped me step into turnouts. My mind wandering, I thought of the firefighters who had responded to my explosion. The turnouts fit me like a glove. Holding the fire hose, the captain described the procedure that would take place in two weeks.

"I'm going to be in there with you, so don't worry about anything in the burning building but holding this hose," he instructed.

There I was surrounded by firefighting equipment, scared, and vulnerable. He was at home in his uniform, throwing his large voice, badge shining in my face, his chest strong and squared. I just wanted to gather up my nine-year-old little-girl self and bolt for my car.

"When the fire starts to crawl over us along the ceiling, you pull this throttle back to get more water flow," he continued his instruction about the hose.

Is he kidding me? What the hell am I doing here?

"OK, great. Like this?" I held the hose up pulling the nozzle open.

On my ride home from the station I continued to question myself. *Am I crazy?* But I wanted to be free. I wanted to face my fears and not be afraid of fire anymore.

On Friday morning the phone rang. It was the captain. I was too scared to answer. He left me a voice mail.

"I just want to check with you about Monday, and go over a few details," he continued. "My students will be in classroom session until noon; we'll break for lunch and then start the live-fire training at 1 p.m. You should plan on arriving at the training tower at 12:30. Call me back and I'll go over more details." He hung up.

I deleted the message and never called him back. I was not going. It was a stupid idea. I'd been through enough.

Allen and I spent Saturday and Sunday boogie boarding in the Pacific, dining on sushi and enjoying our time together. Thoughts of Monday's opportunity haunted me, piercing my peaceful weekend, but I said nothing to Allen.

Monday morning I woke with the levity of an angel waiting for its wings. I felt ready to face my fears! I jumped in my convertible, pushed an angel voices cassette tape in the player and drove through Rancho Santa Fe to the training tower in Poway.

As I pulled up on the tarmac, a firefighter greeted me, "Oh, you must be Lesia. Our captain told us that you *were* going to show up—but he said you never called back."

The stranger in the firefighter uniform seemed flustered.

Suddenly a few bold-looking men in blue uniforms appeared across the tarmac. The captain surfaced from this group. "Well, I'm surprised. I really didn't think you would show up," he shouted from across the blacktop.

"I actually didn't think I would either. But I'm here."

He helped me step into the same yellow turnout fire pants, pulled up the red suspenders and rested them on my shoulders along with his hands and smiled. Could he see my shaken heart?

"Feel OK? You ready to do this?" he asked.

"Yeah, I'm okay … I think."

At any moment I could dash to my car and escape, mail the yellow pants back to him, and forget the whole thing. The captain addressed the sheriff SWAT team standing at near attention with their firefighter gear lying at their feet. I stood alone twenty feet behind him facing the officers. I was shaking. Sheer fear moved through my blood.

"OK, gentlemen, this is the afternoon portion of our live-burn training," he shouted.

What am I doing here? I had no friends with me, no therapist. I was alone, except for God. I prayed my angels would show up to rescue me again if this all went wrong. As much terror as I felt, I was determined to get over my fear of fire.

"Gentlemen, I'd like to introduce you to my crew assisting me this afternoon," the captain continued down his line of his assistants with introductions. Thinking, perhaps hoping, he would forget about introducing me, my mind started to drift to the crippling, horrific memories of the explosion. The captain paused and the voices on the tarmac went silent.

He turned around and looked at me. Startled by the sudden silence, I looked up.

"Now gentlemen, how am I going to introduce Lesia to you?" Now the entire SWAT team tilted their heads from their lineup to get a glimpse of me. *What an asshole!* Looking at him, I whispered to myself: What is this guy doing? He's putting me on the spot.

The captain filled the silence, "Lesia faced her dragon many, many years ago as a little girl. If you get real close to her you will see that he left his mark on her. She lost her battle." He paused and bit his bottom lip, "Today, gentlemen, Lesia is going to face her fear of fire and win her battle." He paused, "So when you see her going in the building, just give her an hoorah or whatever it is you sheriffs do to support her."

I couldn't hold the tears back anymore. *Oh, my God, I can't do this ....*

"You've got ten minutes, gentlemen, to put on your gear. We'll now light the fire in the tower. He instructed a fire-fighter to stack the hay and get the torch ready.

The captain marched over to me, took my hand and casually said something about coming with him to light the pallets.

"I'll walk you into the building and show you what we're going to do before I light the fire," he said.

We approached the building. He had a spring in his step, but I was dragging my courage far behind. He opened the door to the tower. Once inside I saw the option to go down the steps to the basement, or climb up a staircase to a higher level.

I slowly walked inside, fighting the residual smoke smell from previous training burns. My heart raced. The captain climbed down the staircase to the basement with casual movement. I followed, terrified.

I had never had any therapy to deal with the effects of the explosion, my serious burn injury or my emotions. I was drowning in regret that I had even considered re-entering a fire. *This was a huge mistake.* I could feel the panic rising.

"This is what we're going to do: Do you see the straw and hay piled under dry wooden pallets?" the captain said. I nodded back at him. He continued, "We'll set it ablaze; the fire will crawl up the wall and over our heads. And you and I, we'll crouch down on the stairs …." He looked up at me and saw tears rolling down my face.

"Oh? We don't need to do this, Lesia. Maybe this is a bad idea. You don't need to be here." He was then more nervous than I. Men and tears.

He got me out of the building and walked me across the tarmac to my car. "Captain, stop," I managed to say. "I *must* go through with this. I want to be free from fire. I just need you not to let me get burned again," I pleaded through my tears. We stood in the sunlight staring at each other.

"OK, I'm with you. We can do this. I will not get you burned again, I promise you, Lesia. You are safe with me," he committed.

The SWAT team and I suited up on the tarmac while firefighters lit the hay and pallets. I wanted to watch a group go in before us. I wanted to make sure they came out alive, not burned, before I ventured to face my own demon.

The first group came out in awe. We were next. The captain and I got inside the door with hoses in hand. My gloved fingers gripped the hose, my savior should the fire come close.

The door closed behind us, leaving only the space for the hose. The room was dark except the hot amber flame crawling up the wall. The captain was watching the flame as it crawled near us. He nodded at me while he sprayed back the flames.

I was thinking that this was pretty awesome. Here I am sitting in a basement-like room, fire everywhere. He saw that I was alert and present, not freaking out, so he backed us slowly out of the hot blazing room, up the stairs and out the door.

We emerged from the building to cheers and shouts from his students on the tarmac in fire gear, each remembering my story of the dragon.

"Congratulations, you did it!" the captain hugged me. I tore off my mask and gear.

"No, I didn't do it. I have to go back in," I told him.

"Well, you need to sit down, take your gear off, drink some water, and rest a bit." Did he see something happening that I didn't? This was only the start.

The captain sent more students through the burning building. I sat there watching the big strong men hiding their fears as they prepared to enter the fire. They'd had a four-hour class that morning. I had a brief instruction at a fire station and years of scars, my personal reminders of the horrible day that nearly destroyed my family, plus all the anguish of exclusion, rejection, and embarrassment.

"Captain, if we just go into the fire once, do we still get credit?" a student asked.

Wow, these guys were really scared too.

The captain came back to me, "Are you sure you want to go in again?"

"Yeah, sure. Why not," I replied trying to convince myself by putting on a brave front. I truly had to go farther into the fire. I had to feel this deeply, see my angels, peel away the fear and pain that blocked my heart. I made a mental note to myself: *Don't share these deep thoughts with the captain. He won't understand.*

The second time the captain and I entered the burning building, he took me in too far. I knew it. Panic began to overtake my breath. He put me in second behind a training captain. The training captain began to crawl down the stairs into the basement of the building with his hose. I followed closely, too closely, pushing my fear behind me, though I knew enough to stay with him.

Suddenly, I couldn't hold back my panic any longer. My tremendous fear of a nine-year-old on fire again overtook me, consuming me. I heard the roar, then the growl of the beast, the dragon. We couldn't talk or hear each other because the masks feeding oxygen from the tanks strapped to our backs were too loud.

I frantically tried to look up the stairwell for the light, so I could escape, but I only saw smoke and darkness. The captain, my trustworthy stranger, was behind me, his large body blocking the door's crack of light.

Then it happened. I panicked!

I couldn't see anything; I could only hear the fire's roar. I threw my hose down, jumped up (everything you're not supposed to do) and lunged for where I remembered the door to be. As I struggled to clamber over the captain, he grabbed his hose and me and dragged us both out of there. I started to cry as he pulled off my mask and handed me water.

"What happened to you in there?" he asked.

"I felt trapped, captain, when I couldn't see the door. If I could have only seen the door I would've been OK." I was hot. I felt myself falling.

"I think we're done here," he announced, hiding his own fear.

"Please, no, please. I don't want to leave like this. I need to conquer this fear!" I pleaded through my tears.

He hesitated and told me to remove all my outer gear again, drink water and sit down on the tarmac and cool off for awhile. Something told me that he also was talking to himself. What was he getting himself into?

With torn focus the captain ran more students through the fire, often glancing over, waiting for a thumbs-up from me.

I sat on the tarmac, still. My thoughts raced back twenty-four years to the explosion. I asked God to show me strength, show me a sign that my angels who rescued me on that horrible day were now here to help me, again. I begged Him for courage to get through this fire exercise.

"I desperately want my heart to be free. And I'm ready if you're ready, God," I whispered.

The captain approached me and said he'd take me in one more time, if I wanted. "This is your last shot, kiddo. We're ready to wrap this up and call it a day."

"Can it be just you and me this time?" I asked. "I think I got scared with all of the other guys in there and the hoses and everybody screaming."

"Screaming?" his face twisted in question.

Guessing that I was the only one who heard the screams, I realized that the screams had been stuck in my memory for almost a quarter century.

He helped me suit up again. As he tightened my face-mask I could see his eyes through his own mask. Suddenly he looked different to me, like someone I'd known for centuries. My feelings moved from trust to complete safety.

For the first time I saw this man behind his badge.

We entered the burning building again, with the students standing in a half circle watching in amazement. *Courage or craziness?* I'm not sure what they saw. Wooden pallets burning for hours now, it was a lot hotter in there. I see why they needed to finish the training.

We crawled low and sat on the steps leading to the basement—he was on the lower step, and I was on the middle one. There was nothing between the door and me.

Then it happened.

The beams of light came shining through the crack in the ceiling. I sat in awe captivated by the most beautiful swirls of smoke drifting down to where I was sitting. Suddenly angels appeared within the light beams of smoke. I felt my heart being lifted, cradled in the arms of my angels. My prayers, answered. I stared at a vision I remembered seeing years ago in the explosion. They were there, my angels.

The captain patted my thigh and pointed to the fire that was approaching. He signaled me to open my hose nozzle and spray the water on the fire to keep it away. It was getting too close to us.

At that moment, I pointed to the beams of light coming through the ceiling. My angels! I whispered inside my mask. I hadn't shared that in my attempt to conquer my fear, but I was hoping to see my angels again. He had no idea what my personal journey was, nor was he supposed to know. I was convinced he wouldn't understand. Or rather, I didn't want him to think I was nuts, so I didn't press the issue. That was not his duty with me. Being a highly skilled fire captain, he wouldn't let me get burned again. I was safe with him. We both knew that was his gift to me.

Fire blazing overhead, I sat in peace with him for what seemed like a really long time. No fear. No panic. The angels and me. Answered prayers.

The captain continued to spray the flames with water as I sat and stared. He held his gloved hand up signaling the question, "Are you OK?" I returned with a sign of the cross and signaled that I was ready to exit. We stumbled out of the building to a roar of applause from the entire group of SWAT students.

It was a personal moment between God and me, and I had no concept that anyone else got it. The captain smiled and continued his mantra for me to take off my gear including my boots and helmet, sit down and drink tons of water. I sat back on the curb and watched a few more guys come in and out of the building.

I began to feel my body changing. I could feel my heart peeling away layers of fear and pain. I knew I would never be the same again.

The captain approached me and said, "We're putting the fire out. Would you like to slay your dragon?" I packed my gear on quickly, like a pro. I walked over to the door of the burning tower. The captain held the door open while I soaked that room with water. The dragon sizzled as he melted into the ground. I was free.

Like an automaton, I packed up my gear, said a heartfelt thank you and goodbye to the captain and his crews. "That was an extraordinary experience," I said as I gave him a little hug. "I'll take you to lunch for doing this for me."

"Sounds great, I'm going out of town tomorrow for a week in Mexico. I'll call you when I return."

On the drive home, convertible top was down, I was enjoying new emotional freedom. As soon as I opened the door to the house, Allen called.

"How was it?" he asked.

I couldn't find words. Something was changing in me. I told him I was too exhausted to talk. I took a bubble bath, and then lay in bed feeling that my life would never be the same.

The next morning I awakened with a strange heaviness in my heart. I drove to work at the Burn Institute to attend a meeting regarding a fundraiser several fire departments in the county were organizing. I made the mistake of telling the chair of the event about my experience the previous day.

"Whoa, Lesia, that is amazing!" he said. "Can you please share your story with all the guys as an opener to the meeting? That is so inspiring."

As the meeting started, I was introduced. I got ten words out of my mouth when the tears burst through. The screams that I heard, every ounce of pain that my family went through, that the kids at camp go through, every horrific bath scrubbing experience, social rejection, bandage change, my own ripple of scarring, the scarring I have seen—it was all too much. I collapsed in grief. I cried for seven days.

CHAPTER SEVEN

Blind
Dreams

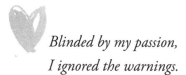

*Blinded by my passion,
I ignored the warnings.*

After a week spent whimpering in a fetal position, drowning in tears, I finally called a therapist. We met at her office. In a few sessions, she taught me to create a box inside my heart and fill it with the pain. "Containerizing" helped me control my tears so they wouldn't overwhelm my day-to-day existence.

This wasn't all that different than my childhood coping mechanisms.

Just after the session I received a call from the fire captain, my new friend. He remembered! I was fearful of my emotions erupting again, so I answered lightly.

"Hey there, Lesia," he said. "So how about lunch?"

At the sound of his voice, the "container" collapsed and every bubble of pain opened up again. Tears dripped on the telephone receiver. "What did we do? Why did I go back into the fire?" I demanded breathlessly. "Please tell me—what was I thinking!" I continued to weep into the phone.

He told me to call him "Bruce." So Bruce and I went for lunch the next day. He answered my questions to clarifying what probably happened in my explosion. This was information my family never spoke of, perhaps never knew. I never knew. Being with him gave me the same sense of strength I'd felt during the burn down. We spent weeks in conversation about fire behavior, burn injuries, the fire service, and difficult calls he had been on.

I finally shared my connection to my angels with Bruce.

Phone conversations turned into lunches, lunches into dinners. We started spending time together talking not about fire but about who we were, our passions and attraction. Watching me go through this process of healing had dislodged something in him too. I had only planned on his keeping me from getting burned again.

The "captain" was falling in love with me. He wasn't the type of guy I would ever have seen myself with. Yet, I was so in awe of what he did on a daily basis. It was what I most feared. And I fascinated him because I had endured some-thing he feared so much. We were bonded.

Dating a fireman was hard. He'd pick me up for a date. I'd climb into his truck. He would've been on duty all night, often at a fire. I could smell smoke. I had to grow accustomed to smoke on a daily basis. It was hard.

One day, we were on the phone while he was at duty. The station tones went off in the background. "Oh, there are the tones. Got to run," he interrupted.

"Quick, before you go, what type of call is it?" I asked, always intrigued.

"A natural gas leak," he blurted out. "I'll call you later." And he hung up.

A gas leak? Is he for real? I had doubts that I could deal with this on a daily basis. The constant adrenaline burst, always about fire, required a lot of adjusting. Yes, the attraction was ironic, but it worked and in all ways was laughably apt. Two years later, on a beautiful fall day on the southern California bluffs, Bruce and I married.

Facing and embracing your fears often come with more gifts than you can imagine.

• • •

Burn camp felt "over," even though I was still at the Burn Institute in San Diego as a spokesperson and to organize and run the camps.

My position was as "Director Support." The title was lofty but the pay was close to minimum wage, even after six years.

Nonetheless, I could impact children's lives, inspire them to heal from their injuries inside and out, and at the same time inspire myself. How lucky I was to do what I could for little wounded hearts. Change was rumbling within the "mountain" in me, though. It was like hearing hurricane warnings and tsunami alarms. The call for transformation reverberated in my soul, yet my passion was such that I ignored the warnings.

Meanwhile, I struggled each month to pay bills. I was doing God's work, but there had to be more. I longed to get closer to the children as they arrived at the hospital, but ironically the Burn Institute's relationship with the large University of California, San Diego Regional Burn Center was strained and they often battled over money and territory.

I never understood the politics, nor was I good at maneuvering through this negativity. My heart was on my sleeve, followed by my thoughts.

Fire departments and the general community mistakenly thought that the two organizations collaborated. I got hushed calls from nurses at the university burn center referring patients to burn camp. They did this under the radar. The nurses and I knew that the disconnect between our employers only hurt children. I was reminded that it was not my position to discuss or clarify the Burn Institute's relationship to UCSD Burn Center—not to the fire community, not to anyone.

Confusion persisted because of missed opportunities continued to pass by to clarify that the Institute was not the hospital. The modus operandi was to gloss over this issue. I cringed at the constant misunderstanding. When a firefighter complimented us by saying, for example, "I'm so glad we are donating all this money to the Burn Institute. If we ever get burned—that's where we are going," I desperately wanted to answer that we were NOT the Burn Center. We are offices, producing fire prevention materials, a fundraising train and, of course, an annual summer burn camp.

But instead I kept quiet, smiled and struggled with the sickly feeling trying to be the loyal employee.

I felt trapped. The burn camp was now becoming the flagship program. But I yearned to be where the children who suffer burn injuries were treated, not at an office with no communication with the Burn Center.

"You will never leave here," my boss said one day. "It's also best if you stay away from the Burn Center personnel." He continually reminded me that dealings with the Burn Center were his to resolve, not mine. The steady drip of this sequestering took its toll on my direction. I was learning how confusion can weaken you, rob your soul from focus and passion. My perception of hypocrisy around me and assumed oppression had me fairly well convinced that any move would mean discord. I was not truly living my heart-centered life; serving my soul's highest path. I could feel my light getting dim inside my being.

Months after summer burn camp was over in 1998, I attended a prestigious international burn conference in Chicago with my boss. In the exhibit hall I ran into the nurse manager from UCSD Burn Center. She happened to be married to Dr. John Hansbrough, its medical director. She was among the people to whom my boss warned me never talk.

I gingerly approached her.

"Wendy, I want you to know that my heart supports burn care teams, any burn team." I was treading in fearful territory. If my boss heard that I had spoken to UCSD personnel, come Monday he'd ask me into his office and want to know everything that was said. The thought exhausted me.

Wendy greeted me professionally yet with the honesty that was her trademark. "Lesia, as long as you are working for Burn Institute you don't support us," she said flatly. Well, this is going well, I grimaced.

Passion in the heart is to be respected and trusted.

I took the risk and continued our conversation.

"I never saw it that way, Wendy. I just want you to know that as a child who was severely burned, my commitment is always to burn care teams. If there is anything I can help you with, please let me know." There I did it. Spoke my heart. Wendy thanked me, we said our goodbyes, and I moved on.

The following afternoon Wendy's husband, Dr. Hansbrough, approached me in the lobby and asked if I would meet him and his wife in their suite for lunch. I agreed.

I ran to my room and threw myself on my bed squealing, "OK, God, what are you up to?" I followed up with a gratitude prayer that whatever was to come would be for my highest good. *What was happening?* I freshened up, swallowed some

Tums, and headed for the elevator. Pushing the button for the 46th floor was like heading for heaven. A new job?

As the elevator doors opened, I peeked around for my boss. With my shifting sensations, the walls seemed to open and close as I passed each door, glancing at the suite numbers.

I knocked on the door at the very end. *The door to my future?* I giggled with God, but was really feeling nauseous. I wanted to run, yet my heart danced. *What did they want of me? A job offer? A hostage taking?* I was paralyzed with fear at what would happen if I left my position at the Burn Institute. I wondered just now how many times had he reminded me that I would be nothing without the burn camp.

"Come in, Lesia," Wendy opened the door with purpose. The suite was massive with a view overlooking nearly the entire city of Chicago. Dr. Hansbrough stood up from the large round dining table and extended his gentle surgeon hand. He was a brilliant burn surgeon, Harvard graduate, and responsible for cutting edge research with growing artificial skin. He was not only world renown for professional accomplishments, but also a father figure for many severely burned patients whose lives he had saved. My respect for him was enormous.

Handsome yet gruff, Dr. Hansbrough was clearly more comfortable in an operating room or a research laboratory than any social setting. He quickly acknowledged the work I had done with the children at burn camp and my good reputation. Coming from this legend, the recognition was huge. He was not known for compliments.

That moment so filled me that I could very easily have turned on my heels and departed happy.

After our introductions, we chatted briefly about the weather, the burn conference, and then lunch arrived at the door.

Receiving a tribute from an impressive admirer can reinforce, push and encourage brave steps toward growth and the awakening to what's important in life. Keep stepping forward.

Dr. Hansbrough wasted no time. "Are you happy at the Burn Institute?" he asked.

"Not really, I'd like to work more directly with the burn patients," I blurted out.

Dr. Hansbrough looked down, taking a sip of his tea, and then continued resolutely, "Lesia, I admire the work you do and what you have accomplished. I want you to come work for us. We need you at the Burn Center; my patients need you."

I nearly collapsed. *The* Dr. Hansbrough admired *me? Don't ever wake me! I'm living my dream.* With that, he then offered me a full-time position supporting the patients and their families as they were admitted to the Burn Center. The position would come with full health benefits, a salary triple what was I was making at the Burn Institute, sick leave, vacation time, everything I didn't have with my current employer.

Hellooooo, God, Are you watching this? I sank in my chair and fought back tears of gratitude.

Tears in front of Dr. and Mrs. Hansbrough? I felt so unprofessional. Did they realize how magical it was to hear my dream coming true? I accepted their initial offer, acknowledging we had a lot of details to work out. Lunch was served. I barely ate a thing as I elevated off my chair, towering above the city of Chicago, dining with the King of Burn Care.

We said our goodbyes with a promise that when we returned to San Diego in a few days they would start the process of making a formal contract offer. We agreed that nothing was to be mentioned until I received the contract and was in a position to give my current employer proper allotted notice that I was leaving.

As soon as I closed the door of their suite, I raced to the elevator with tears gushing from my eyes. I was breathing heavily from the excitement of breaking free of an unhealthy situation and into the arms of God's path for me. After a squealing call of glee to my husband, I considered the dreaded duty of "giving notice" at the Burn Institute. It would be horrible, but the feeling of being unshackled, free of the arena I'd been working in for years was like touching the gates of heaven. My dream had arrived.

When an amazing opportunity presents itself, it is a soul's awakening. Learn to trust your path. Don't look back, unless you dare.

I needed a few trusted others to guide me through this process of resignation—God, my husband Bruce, Dave, and a fire chief I had always admired came to mind. My angels' boss, God, would never fail me.

I stopped by Fire Station 28 to discuss my new opportunity with Dave, my steadying angel. It's always a risk visiting a firehouse for a friendly chat; one never knows what type of call the firefighters have just returned from. I took my chances. I was so giddy that it felt as if stars twinkled about me as I walked into the firehouse.

Dave knew of my personal silent struggles at the Burn Institute, so I was guaranteed his matched passion for my career path. He knew what this offer meant to my heart and pocketbook, yet he had the distance and wisdom to recognize that leaving my boss would not be easy.

"Be careful, Lesia," Dave warned. "Your boss will not like this. To him, it means much more than losing you. Your departure will raise a lot of questions. Besides, maybe UCSD is just playing a game with you, using you as a political pawn. You are a golden goose. You know that, right?"

"Good grief, Dave. Can't you just be happy for me—about my new job offer—and not be so cautious? This is my dream job!" I sang.

"I'm happy for you, Lesia, but I question what the fallout will do to you." This was so confrontational, close to an argument. Would this be the first we'd ever had?

"But Dave, am I not allowed to further my career? Working four days a week, getting paid for two and for only $6.50 an hour? Come on! It's insulting. Besides, with my new position at UCSD I can now quit my other two jobs and work with the burn team. This is heaven sent!" I cried.

Dave looked down and softly said, "I just care about you, Lesia, and don't want you to get hurt." I drove away, deflated. Not sure if the tightening in my stomach was because of that or fear that he was right. That was Warning Number One.

There is no way of knowing how unhealthy a situation is while you are in it. Sure, you have a sense it is happening, you feel icky in the situation, but you become adept at rationalizations for why you stay. Feeling stuck can build assumptions that you are no good without the situation. Once free, there is a period of peeling away the assumptions.

Before the job offer, I had made plans to have a reconstructive medical procedure. My surgery had been on the books for months. Long before this career opportunity surfaced. Recovery was brutal but gave me a lot of time to think about my new direction. This glimpse of freedom made it very clear that I needed to leave and be free to create my future. At the same time, imagining the new me as well as the lives and opportunities that I could touch was euphoric and scary.

Meanwhile the wheels slowly turned through the large university's hiring process. I spoke with Dr. Hansbrough briefly at one of the pre-hire paper signings.

"When are you giving your resignation over there?" he asked.

"In a few days sir, as soon as my new position is secure here," I replied.

"Call me as soon as you resign. I want to hear how it goes." He dashed off to surgery. This was another unrecognized warning—Warning Number Two.

After I healed from my surgery and the position at the Burn Center was secure with a written offer of everything Dr. Hansbrough had promised me, I was ready to report back to work and to resign.

The day arrived.

On my way to the office I stopped at a random church to pray. God is everywhere, right? A church is a church. I found an empty pew and let it pour out. "God, please give me the strength to resign with ease and grace … " I then got in my car and called my favorite fire chief for coffee.

"Chief Ghio, can you meet me for coffee? I need some advice."

Over coffee I shared with Chief Ghio my offer from UCSD, my dream come true. "Well, Lesia, this is great news, an excellent opportunity for your career. You must take it," he assured me. "But I didn't know the relationship with the Burn Center was not good. I always thought that they worked closely," he claimed with questioning crimp in his brow. "What is the real relationship?"

Chief Ghio's question was my Warning Number Three. "It's not so good," I dodged. What I really wanted were his blessings, but I asked, "Should I tell my boss where I'm going?"

"Yes, he will find out anyway. Best he hear it from you." The chief smiled, hugging me goodbye. "Call me when it's over. You may need to talk. I'm here for you, Lesia."

I walked into my office, smiled at my co-workers and got a box from the storage room. I laid it next to my desk, and then popped my head in my boss's office. With a dry mouth I asked if we could talk.

He and I plus my immediate supervisor, met in his office. My boss was still standing as I sat down. My sweaty palms hidden in my suit coat pocket were already over-reacting—or rather predicting. I had no idea how unhealthy this relationship had become. Nor was I capable of foreseeing what my departure would mean—I just knew I had to leave and keep looking forward.

"So what's up?" he asked, folding his arms over his chest and looming over me.

"I think it's time for me to move on. I'm giving you my official three week notice," I said, handing him my official letter of resignation.

"What? No! Why? You can't leave us!" his voice growled trying to hide the shock and anger. "We need to talk about this."

"I think it's time," I said—with my voice strengthening. "I need to be able to support myself without working three jobs."

My voice got even stronger as I spoke. Meanwhile, my inner guide, God's voice, said, "Ease up, my child. Easy now

… go with grace and ease. That's why you prayed." *Yes, thank you God.*

"So where are you going?" he asked now with his hands on his hips. Remembering Chief Ghio's words, I told my boss that I was going to work at the UCSD Burn Center.

I swear that smoke blew from his ears. I was scared of what was coming next.

"Well … you've done quite well for yourself, I see… " Before I could respond, he turned on his heels and opened the door. He escorted me back to my desk where he told me to gather my personal belongings off my desk.

He asked for my office keys and escorted me out the back door. I sat in my car and exhaled. It was over. I hadn't expected that I would leave at that moment, there were so many goodbyes I wanted to give, work to be completed but the deed was done. I was now free to create the life I wanted. At least that's what I thought.

Dr. Hansbrough had wanted me to call as soon as I officially resigned. I dialed his cell number from my car.

"Well congratulations," Dr. Hansbrough said with a little excitement. "How did he take it?" That seemed a strange question, which I might have recognized as Warning Number Four, but I didn't.

My new navy suit looked perfect and appropriate for my first day of work at the Burn Center. The next two weeks were heaven—working with the burn team, meeting the nurses, the residents, learning the protocols, responsibilities and boundaries of my new dream position, and yes, embracing the patients.

I felt God's love inside of me each moment of the day. It was everything I wanted. I belonged there. I was *home*. Not until those early days at the Burn Center did the depth of how much I needed to leave the Burn Institute hit me.

This kind of revelation is common with flight from any form of psychological abuse. I had stayed as long as I did because the children I connected with through burn camp nearly sustained me. They kept me on higher ground. These children were treated at the Burn Center, though. I could still maintain relationships with them—see them in the clinic, become more involved in their journey. Or so I thought.

My husband and I spent several nights over dinner discussing how blessed I was to get this position and how excited my future was becoming.

Then the nightmare started.

Two weeks later slandering "letters" to the CEO of the Medical Center began arriving. Soon it was a flood. They came from many different fire chiefs, union leaders, and other people from the community.

"Why did you hire Lesia Cartelli using state funds, when the Burn Institute was providing those services for free?" "Lesia Cartelli is duplicating services that the Burn Institute provides" … and so on. The sentences in the letters made no sense, because my new work was entirely different. Also the sentences in the letters were all exactly the same. Something was weird.

This couldn't be happening! The cruelty of a man who has lost control took the form of a vicious letter writing campaign.

The hospital administration at a high level was disturbed but still very supportive. "It simply shows that you were a star employee," the CEO said to me. However, the letters continued.

"We received another nasty letter today, but don't worry. He is just angry he lost a good employee," Dr. Hansbrough mentioned between patients.

Each day newly burned patients flew in on helicopters and mothers wept in my arms as their child endured intense pain while clinging to life. The burn team was swamped with the work of saving people but the nasty letters kept coming. It was clear to everyone, however, that the Burn Center was where I belonged.

"Give it some time. The letters will stop," the Director of Government Relations at the medical center assured me, in yet another meeting with the top brass at the university.

With each letter, I was pulled into another meeting, confronted with new questions as to why these letters were coming. I had no answers. The nurses who had been so supportive began to draw away from me, in fear that association would cause their job uncertainty.

My energy and my self-esteem shrank by the day; my dream eroded a little more with every letter. Just as bad, some of the letters were from the Who's Who in the firefighting community. When my husband and I went out socially, I was bombarded with questions and judgments from people in the fire service, the same fire service my husband was a member.

Each day brought something worse.

"The medical center's upper management strongly suggests that you refrain from attending social gatherings until this 'inflamed situation' blows over," Dr. Hansbrough told me on our way to a patient's room.

My new husband Bruce, a fire captain with the San Diego City Fire Department, was very dedicated in his career path, and very social. How could I not attend a gathering?

The effects spread. Bruce was next in line for the gold badge, interviewing to become a Battalion Chief. He had all the credentials, experience, knowledge, skills and command to lead a battalion of seven fire stations, plus three decades of service on the force. He walked into his scheduled interview, prepared, and optimistic. On his interview panel were his supervisors and various division chiefs. One member in all her chief uniform brass, sat behind the interview table. She was also a board member for my former employer. Bruce was denied another promotion.

Bruce would ultimately endure five pass overs for battalion chief and six more interviews before becoming chief, well after the events to come.

Then there were calls and letters from the children from burn camp I had started: "Lesia, where are you?" "Why did you leave us?" "Why won't you talk to me?" These handwritten messages from the children broke my heart and my spirit, particularly because my new employer forbad me to answer them. The university was trying to limit my exposure to retaliation, but my dream was fast becoming a nightmare.

In the middle of all this, *ABC 20/20* filmed a segment about my husband and how we met. The producer shot a question over the bow.

"What happened to you at the Burn Institute? Why are you not there anymore?" she asked.

"Why do you ask?" I flinched.

"Well, Lesia, we are an investigative news agency. When we were looking for you to do the story about your amazing work, we called them and they were very mysterious. They wouldn't tell us where you had moved onto," the producer Juliet shared.

Oh, no! I needed to tell her. I glossed over the painful parts, jumping to how UCSD assured me they would take care of me and protect me and how much I loved my new job.

"Lesia, I've been with ABC twenty years. My husband is the CFO of a large bank in Manhattan. You need an attorney," she admonished.

"Thanks, Juliet, but it'll pass over. I'm taking the Buddhist way, the high road, not buying into the energy," I lied. Every letter and social restriction crushed me a little bit more.

"Lesia, every good Buddha knows when to get out her sword," Juliet cautioned. "Find a good attorney." Warning Number Five.

I changed the conversation and we wrapped up the filming.

Arriving at work the following day I learned that the university had now received 38 accusatory letters. They each defamed the university and me, and they cc'd many political figures in the State of California. After only nine months of my dream job, the university had had enough.

Administrators called me into Dr. Hansbrough's office (while he was vacationing in Hawaii) and laid me off effective immediately, telling me that the funding for my position was gone, despite my position was not based on grant money.

My former Burn Institute boss had won the battle against me, the battle the university and Dr. Hansbrough told me to ignore. So much for protecting me! Broken and shattered, I walked out of the medical center in the pouring rain. It was as though the heavens were crying with me. As I drove away there it was … a massive full six-color rainbow. Maybe my spirit knew I would be OK, but it sure didn't feel like it. My car carried my battered soul and slowly rolled me home.

Not until six weeks' worth of my face planted on my tear soaked pillow did I

Losing our way is really not being lost at all. Feeling lost is a time of honor and an opportunity to trust where we are in our journey. Feelings of uncertainty are there to teach us to open our eyes, move gently and slowly, but move forward.

turn my phone back on and open my drapes acknowledging I had to go on. I had to go on not so much for me, but for my husband. He was my rock. He was my everything.

It was pouring down rain one early evening while Bruce and I were having dinner. There was a knock on our front door. It was a fireman friend, a guy named Kurt, asking to speak to us.

"Lesia, excuse me for getting involved but I can't bear you lost your job. We at the firehouse can't stand by and watch this happen to you any longer. I have a name of a good lawyer for you. You must call him."

Reflecting on the television producer's advice earlier, I took the number and made an appointment for the following week. As painful as the arena was and with my reputation spiraling out of control, support was rushing in the backdoor, some of it anonymously. I received greeting cards pledging support, "Keep fighting, Lesia, we are all behind you." "Many believe in you." "Keep your head up." All with no signature.

My situation was a political hot potato; I wasn't the only one afraid.

My phone rang early one morning. It was one of the fire chiefs. "Lesia, I have a cassette tape of a recent fire department meeting where the request was made that we all needed to write letters and stop you from working at UCSD. As the note taker of the group, I record the meetings. I think you need to take this cassette tape to your attorneys. I'm happy to give it to you, I feel so bad this is happening."

"Whoa, gosh … thank you," I stammered.

I was no stranger to the negative energy of lawsuits since one had pierced my childhood. This time was different. The betrayal had burned a hole more painful than my seared skin years ago.

This lawsuit, which lasted two years, added its own destructive drag. The mess broadened when it deposed thirty-eight fire chiefs, union leaders, and university officials. I never spoke to Dr. Hansbrough after I was laid off and felt that the university might have warned him to stay clear of me. However, he turned over handwritten personal journals to my attorneys stating how hard it was for him to watch me go through this. Then, unrelatedly, another tragedy occurred.

In the middle of my lawsuit against the Burn Institute, Dr. Hansbrough, who suffered from depression, drove one hour east of San Diego, and in a deserted, hot dusty desert he shot a bullet into his heart. The world of burn care mourned deeply; so did I.

In drying my tears of mounting stress from filings, depositions, depression, rejection, discovery and lies, my thoughts flashed to the little

We never learn about ourselves in times of comfort. It's in the deepest of sorrow or pain that we must embrace our soul. Sometimes that means crawling into bed to nap while hugging ourself to sleep, a walk in nature, or sipping a cup of hot tea. Honor where one is—because the period won't last long.

faces at burn camp, my faces of angels. To survive the lawsuit's stress. I needed to allow the healing to begin. I reflected back on surviving my burn injury. How did I do that? I'm not sure.

Yet I was sure I had power and light buried deep in me somewhere that I needed to find and use for the good. I needed to touch the lives of young girls who were damaged as much as I needed to touch my own life.

In the middle of my healing my husband and I purchased another home and I poured my energy into remodeling it myself. Home Depot employees smiled as I sauntered by daily in recognition of "another project"—or trying to repair the one I had started the day before. What I was really trying to repair was my heart, my career, my life, my hope, and my dream. All shattered. Home Depot didn't have an aisle that sold souls.

Whatever we plant in life will grow and thrive if nurtured, watered, and fertilized. Much like our souls, this manifestation takes time, during which hope reigns whether we realize it or not.

The house was transforming beautifully, but I was still in shambles. There were days when my intense sorrow over losing my opportunity to help children crippled me. I'd lost not only the children from my burn camp and my stellar reputation, but the divestiture of my dream job at the Burn Center removed me from many more children.

I planted flowers, bushes, bulbs; whatever would grow, I planted it. One day I even came home with a tree. My husband just shook his head. I wanted to hang a sign around my neck, "Healing in Process, Do Not Disturb." He knew I was trying to recover but he also needed his wife back. And, of course, he had his own fallout from all this to deal with.

While Bruce and I hung onto that mantra, our back-yard became lush. There is a lot of power and beauty in planting flowers, bulbs, bushes, and even a tree.

After a few failed attempts at mediation, the case prepared for trial. Just weeks before trial the Burn Institute and I settled. The settlement check laid on my dresser for days before I deposited it into my bank. Money, at any amount truly doesn't heal.

CHAPTER EIGHT

Angel Faces Delivered

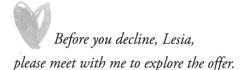

Before you decline, Lesia,
please meet with me to explore the offer.

Our new house gradually became our home. However, as I overturned soil and lowered plants into the ground, my feelings of rejection and betrayal remained excruciating. By then in my forties, I was no stranger to these feelings and should have somehow developed strategies for overcoming them. Yet, on the inside I was still the same isolated, mortified little nine-year-old.

In the garden I pushed, cried and pleaded with myself to *heal through creativity*, but nothing was happening ... or nothing *seemed* to be happening. One day, I heard a whisper of faith within me: *"Why can't you create your own 'good' from this 'bad'?"*

I knew I must progress somehow but I was very fearful. What about the burn camp's shortfalls about which I felt increasingly guilty? What about my reputation in the burn community? All the lies! I really could not handle more humiliation or rejection. And for sure, I couldn't bear more betrayal, the hurt still made me shake and cry.

My anguish was like deep packed soil. It hadn't come from a single incident. Inseparable from me, pain had accumulated over my whole life. I could think of no one to ask for help. Feeling so alone forced me to stop and look at myself. Where else? Some people don't do this, but doesn't it all boil down to oneself ultimately anyway?

Our tendency during acute pain is to think of ourselves as victims, to concentrate on how others have wronged us. However, a lot of growth can come from accepting that we all play a part in whatever happens to us, be it .001 percent or much greater.

So I asked myself what was my responsibility? What could I have done differently?

Nothing.

Yet gnawing at me was the revelation that had hit me two years before when my volunteer friend Dave and I saw those dejected teenage girls walk by with downcast gazes. I had known then that I wasn't doing enough, not fulfilling my promise—not serving my soul's purpose. Wasn't there a way to see that revelation as the engine behind all that had occurred since?

The mess I crawled out of—had to have a blessing leading to now.

What could I do about my situation? No choices seemed to be coming from outside me, so whatever my future might be was all up to me, me and my angels. We had to sow the seeds right into that deep pain and grow the pain up and out.

I could start an intensive retreat for adolescent girls—welcoming those who wanted to embrace their pain, heal, and move on with their life, yet didn't know how. The irony was that I intended to invite these young girls into the exact place I was in that moment. Nevertheless, I felt that I could teach them everything I knew or point them to others who had those skills.

I was confident that whatever I didn't have, I could find. I was blessed with having a few strong, healthy women in my life, women I trusted and admired who possessed that rare nectar for healing. Everyone has gifts, and I had been fortunate to attract people whose gifts would help traumatized young girls find their power. Bold thoughts!

All this ran through my mind and heart. Even with all the years at the Burn Institute's camps and my short time at the Burn Center, I felt I had only scratched the surface of my capability. I kept digging. I refused to waste the pain of the last few years.

I knew my gifts were inside of me; I just needed to coax them to the surface. Abruptly, excitement about this idea swept in!

As I hauled more rocks in the backyard to realize my latest garden idea—a waterfall—more thoughts trickled in. My birthday was approaching. As my idea for helping adolescent girls transform their pain percolated, I began to realize I had two birthdays, one when I was born and another the day of the explosion, a painful birthday of my soul—a deep internal soul decision that pushed me to survive fire.

We all have a few "birth" days in our life—our physical birthday followed by birthdays of awakening. The explosion of awakening. The additional birth might be marked by the death of a loved one, a birth of a child, a traumatic accident, or any turning point in your path where your life becomes dramatically different, where you handle the situation in a decidedly new way. You might think of these as contracts you've made with your soul, sometimes on a level you can't see, but you feel.

This interval in my life was a birthday. This awakening took months but as it sank in I knew that if I chose to, my own wounded spirit could discover strength and courage.

Through my pain, healing, and passion I could launch a unique retreat for adolescent girls to face their injuries, uncover the light within them and help them build a life they never thought possible. With the help of my strong women friends, we could drive a successful retreat, rerouting pain to positive action for the girls—that was my clear path. I was on it. It was time to open my internal gifts and eat celebratory cake!

I needed money to make this program happen.

Feeling a new sense of hope, I jumped on the treadmill at the gym. A woman I knew only casually stepped onto the machine next to me. We started to chat and she began to tell me that she was bored with her life. How could you be bored with life, I thought? I haven't been bored since 1972. I

Thoughts are powerful, manifesting the moment that lies before you. What you think expands in your world.

began to tune her out as I increased my pace, but she continued about needing something to do with her life.

"How about rocking babies at the hospital," I pounded out between breaths, "or volunteer at the trauma intervention program (TIP)." I explained that I had been a volunteer at TIP for a few years and loved it.

"Do you think they are a good organization to donate to?" she asked. She explained that her family had a well-funded foundation and she was looking for a cause to donate to.

There it was! I hit the stop button on my treadmill and said, "OK, let's talk!" I told her about my idea and my passion behind it.

Ten days later, I received a big check in the mail. I had the money! Just like that. The woman I had first dismissed stepped up to rock this baby—me. A kind of angel herself, she recognized my passion and trusted my vision. This is the power of thought, like I said. I will always be grateful for her believing in me.

I called a facility in the local mountains, which I had rented for burn camp in the past. Securing a long weekend in August, I started to design the program. I needed a name for my new idea. Reflecting on the three adorable little girls at burn camp who had asked me to play in the pool (right after I'd noticed the sad older girls) gave me an idea. I had seen their expectant faces as "angel faces"—the name came rushing in—Angel Faces.

In the busy days of learning how to acquire a nonprofit status, I received a call from Victoria, the nurse manager of the University of California, Irvine, Regional Burn Center and a board member of the Orange County Burn Association.

"I'd like to interview you for a position we have. It's the executive director for our nonprofit affiliated with our burn center," Victoria offered.

Is this a joke? The searing pain of betrayal I'd just been through between the two institutions was still smoldering. This felt like a test. I trusted no one.

"Well, thank you for considering me, Victoria, I'm flattered but I'm not interested in the position," I replied.

"Before you decline, Lesia, please meet with me to explore the offer," Victoria pleaded. "I'm willing to drive down from Orange County to meet with you."

Sifting through fear of another political mess on the one hand and staying open to opportunities on the other, I chose the latter. Besides, she was coming to me. I knew nothing of UCI Regional Burn Center.

"OK, I can meet you next week but only for an hour." My rules this time. Setting boundaries was key. I was getting my power back, yet still vulnerable. I couldn't risk another broken dream.

Our lunch meeting went smoothly. Overlooking the harbor, Victoria explained that they were looking for an executive director at the Orange County Burn Association on the property of the UCI Burn Center. I shared my goal of launching Angel Faces, saying that my passion was to fill a need in this country. I also told her that I was in the early stages of applying for my 501c3 non profit status.

"Well, we are a 501c3 non profit. Why don't you accept our offer as executive director, and you can launch Angel Faces under our non-profit status, collect a salary, benefits and write your schedule?" Victoria smiled.

"Victoria, I have to be honest with you, I have just been through a very tough time with a political situation between two organizations and I'm not interested in stepping back into that arena." I dreaded having to share this but knew I needed to be honest.

"I know all about that, Lesia. We actually received a letter during that time explaining that you were a 'disgruntled employee' and urging us never to hire you." She continued, "That letter told us more about the sender than you. We are not interested in politics. We want you. We are very familiar with your worth."

This was good to hear but I still felt wary. I sipped my tea. "I need time to discuss this with my husband and do a little soul searching. I'm sure you understand," I vacillated.

We said our goodbyes, and I dropped Victoria at the train. She seemed sincere and caring. I liked her. Yet I was scared.

We met a few more times. I traveled to Orange County, and noted that the job would come with a long commute. Still, it was a steady salary, a place to fledge Angel Faces and perhaps a place to heal. After meeting with the Board of Directors and the burn team, I decided to accept the position in early June 2003.

Dr. Marianne Cinat was the medical director of the UCI Regional Burn Center. She was passionate, warm, and real. She and her team welcomed me with open arms, smiles, and clear intentions to strengthen the support for her patients.

I was trusting my new path yet leery. Was I being set up again? I poured myself into the position as executive director, strengthening support programs while creating new ones for burn patients, including my new Angel Faces program.

Nine months later, I launched our first four day long Angel Faces retreat. Nine girls came from all across the country. I wanted this retreat to be everything burn camp was not. There was to be no material gifts, no giveaways, and no pretending their lives were "normal."

My goal was to help them on the big issues, as I knew them. How did they handle the staring and teasing they dealt with daily? Peeking back into my adolescent path, I knew the volume of humiliation was too great and unrelenting for most people who have suffered from burn/trauma injuries to grapple with.

I had no one to talk to as a hurt teenager and had often felt the girls' hunger for a cadre of friends, maybe just one who looked like me. I wasn't the only traumatized girl who had protected her family and herself by "stuffing." Almost all these kids avoid the helplessness that might result from "opening up."

I felt strongly that pushing these girls with serious burn injuries to look deep into their pain would give them a soft place to fall. From there we could build a stronger sense of who they were, aside from having a burn injury trama. This ambition meant achieving a delicate balance. I was really excited, but it was also very scary.

The girls began arriving at the site. I placed a wobbly table at the door and assigned a volunteer to check them in as they arrived. The first girl shuffled up the path with her parents and close behind, my team of volunteers.

"Hello there, Michelle," my nervous voice cracked. She peeked up from her contorted face. I offered my hand. "Welcome, nice to meet you." Michelle offered up her hand which had only a split of two fingers.

"Hi, nice to meth yu," she struggled with her enunciation. Michelle was born with Mobius Syndrome, a rare neurological disorder.

Her father stepped forward, "Thank you so very much for welcoming our daughter to your camp," he said, shielding his wife who was hiding behind him.

"Retreat, it's a retreat," I emphasized. I needed no association with the camps. Oh no, I could feel the pain of my burn camp days resurfacing. Shoving it down, I pulled my energy up into my higher chakra and continued with a warm smile, "You are so very welcome, Mr. Rodriguez. We will do our best to teach her a lot of skills and give her the tools to improve her life."

As other girls were arriving, I motioned for another volunteer to show Michelle and her parents where she would sleep. Then came the process of separating the parents from their daughter whom they'd protected her whole life.

As each new girl arrived, my path became clearer. Once they were all gathered in the living room of the facility, I opened up the weekend.

"Girls, welcome home." Fighting back tears I continued, "We are all here because of a common thread. A thread of having an experience of a severe trauma or having been born with a disfiguring anomaly that left us looking different." With that I could see the girls chancing glances at each other. I continued, "It is my prayer for you this weekend that you realize this is your safe place to fall, a place where you can finally begin to heal, to learn about love and ultimately embrace where you are today in your young lives and build upon where you stand."

I saw a few smiles. "This is a place where you are safe. A place where you will find friends for life."

I could hear exhaling throughout the room.

"It's up to you how much work you are willing to do for yourself this weekend. The choice is yours. I promise you that my beautiful team of volunteers and I will give you our best. It's completely up to you if you want to absorb what you hear and how much you are willing to participate in your own healing."

I took a big breath. Standing in silence in front of a group of hungry eyes, I thanked God that I made it here after three years of hell. I prayed that God would give me all the words to share with the girls for the next four days. *I needed this as much as the girls.*

I spent the remainder of the day going over the schedule and logistics and helping the girls and volunteers settle in. The girls didn't know each other and breaking the

Listening deeply to our intuition, the whispers from above and around us, we can begin the process of clarity and healing. Welcome this deep softness of knowing we are right where we need to be.

ice was a challenge. Dinner came and went with only a few quiet conversations at the table. Once back at the house, we settled into our rooms for the night. I rang the chimes, and then a few volunteers and I popped into the girls' semi-private rooms to wish them good night.

As I crawled into my own bed, I wondered if the retreat was really the right thing to do. I already knew the answer.

I woke at dawn to check on the girls. Opening the door to the first room, I found empty beds. I dashed to the second room and flung open the door: empty. By the time I reached the third room my heart was palpitating. Did they all run away? A healing retreat? What was I thinking? Fearing the worst, I pushed on the third door to find something blocking it on the other side. As I began to force it open, I peered through the crack.

All nine girls were snuggled together, sound asleep, mattresses on the floor, sharing blankets, pillows and a common wound. A slumber party! The sleepover they always wanted to be invited to that never happened, until now.

At that moment in the dawn hours of a warm August, grace squelched my fear. I was filled with happiness. This was the right path!

"Good morning, Angels," I whispered through the crack. Out of the lines of their mottled scars, soft smiles appeared, "Ummm, good morning," and then they drifted back to sleep.

I'm not certain who healed more those few days of the retreat. During the previous three years I had often felt pangs of terror, believing that I had lost the connection with the children I came to love at burn camp. But creating this retreat was pushing me into a path of faith—I was right where I needed to be.

I would meet new girls who needed my help and those new girls were with me, in this room—without the politics that can taint healing, stump growth, and squelch creativity.

During the retreat, a group from a distant high school arrived to share the facility for their own retreat. This was difficult. I had reassured the girls upon arrival that this was a safe place. Now we were faced with sharing mealtimes with 200 "normal" looking high school students. The facility had staggered meal times so as we were finishing our meal, the high school students pushed into the cafeteria. Staring and whispers began to pour over to our group.

A girl named Crystal stood up from her dessert and bolted out the closest door, our licensed therapist, Charlotte, and myself on her heels.

We found her sitting on a rock tucked away near our house. "Crystal, why did you run?" Charlotte asked.

"You don't understand …" she sobbed. "At school, I eat in the school office because I can't handle the other students staring and teasing me. I never go into the cafeteria at school, never."

Charlotte and I shared a look of compassion followed by a whisper between us committing to work on this with Crystal. My mind filled with questions: *Why does her school allow her to not eat in the cafeteria, feeding her fear? Don't they know that they are enabling her blockage to avoid what feels uncomfortable? Why don't they address the issue?*

The next day as a team we focused our energy on tools to help Crystal and the other girls push through to cultivate a stronger self image and confidence. Breathe, stand tall, make eye contact and trust yourself was the message we rehearsed.

Getting Crystal to be comfortable in a room full of teenagers was doable but she needed to "want" this goal. We all need to "want" to change before we can begin to push ourselves to learn anything.

Dinner time rolled around the next night. We sat at our tables, enjoying the grilled cheese. I noticed Crystal was the first in line to eat, probably so she could be the first to leave. I knew this behavior all too well; it was my own at age fifteen. She was finishing her dessert when the boisterous students arrived again. She looked at me across the table, stood and bolted. Ugh. This was going to take some work and time.

The last night while dining in the cafeteria—here they came, the students. I looked at Crystal and mouthed, "Breathe … stay … breathe. You're fine," I whispered. With the other girls noticing, I could see their chests rise and fall in solidarity.

Crystal finished her dessert. When she looked at me for strength, I said, "You're finished. Are you ready to take your plates to the cleanup station?"

She looked at me frozen with horror.

"C'mon follow me." I stood up, walked to her chair and led her winding through all the tables to the cleanup station. I looked at the high school students periodically, with Crystal still on my heels. I smiled at them nodding my head with hello falling from my breath.

Crystal and I returned to the table with cheers from the other girls.

"I did it!" Crystal threw her hands in the air. "I did it … I can't believe I did it … I walked all through the students, feeling OK! I'm going back to my school and tell them I don't need to eat in the office anymore!"

At the close of the retreat, there were tearful goodbyes, noticeable changes and heads looking up to their future, not down on the pavement.

All the girls had left, but as we were packing up, there was a knock on the door. It was Michelle's father, with tears in his eyes. Uh-oh, I thought. He had picked up his daughter over an hour before. Now he was back? Had something terrible happened en route home? Hearing stories for three days about the horrific accidents the girls had endured, we were freshly reminded that life can change in an instant.

"May I see Lesia, please," I heard him ask through his gasps. I set a box of supplies down and headed to the front door.

"I'm here," I gently smiled, "Is there something wrong, Mr. Rodriguez?"

"No, heavens no, Lesia, it's about my daughter ... I want to thank you and your volunteers. My daughter ... she is so happy. I have never seen her like this, ever. She is talkative, laughing, and smiling. I had to turn the car around and come thank you personally. You have changed my daughter's life," he cried right there in my arms.

Later that afternoon, on my drive home, I too wept. My purpose was very clear and validated now. I couldn't stop for pain or fear anymore. There was much work to be done.

Arriving home from the retreat is always a challenging transition. My heart flayed open. Eyes drained of tears, visions of God's grace running through my veins, and a week of miracles cradled with pain. I am home.

Yet my real home is in my life's work. Bruce is there waiting for me, my rock, my grounding force. Somewhere in between, I'm my best.

CHAPTER NINE

Risks and Rewards

Whatever loss I had suffered,
I was never going to leave me.

I reveled in my position at the Orange County Burn Association (OCBA). Working so closely with the burn team restored my faith that working relationships between burn centers and nonprofits can work.

At the UC Regional Burn Center in Irvine, California, Dr. Cinat led an extraordinary team of caring, loving burn-care specialists. The team welcomed me and called upon me with appreciation and support for my position and who I was as a person.

With passing years, I had a few more retreats behind me, each strengthening the program and the results. I was content yet growing, and I began to feel that Angel Faces needed its own identity. Every time I presented about OCBA's programs the questions from the audience were always about Angel Faces. I felt guilty—I was there to present more than Angel Faces, yet the audience must have seen where my passion was.

In the spring of 2006 I sat in my beautiful office in Irvine, glancing out at jacaranda trees that filled the view with lavender. My position was very nurturing, yet I felt a nagging urge for change. I entertained leaving at my next contract renewal in six months.

The first step toward change is when we open our eyes and look for the messages that nudge us forward. Do not be afraid of change. However, recognize that the phrase "change is healthy" usually comes from someone whom your change does not impact.

A week after the close of another successful retreat, my assistant popped her head in my office.

"Lesia, may I speak with you openly?" Bianca asked.

"Sure, come in." I pulled away from my computer and gave her my full attention.

"Please excuse me for being so personal—I know you are my boss and all but … well. I have been working for you for one year now, and I've only seen one side of your work here—until I saw you in action at the retreat.

Lesia, I saw a side of you that was so happy, in your element, while doing amazing work with what you taught the girls. Have you thought of just doing that full time and not working here?" Her voice was gentle and tentative.

Good grief, where was Bianca going with this, I wondered? She wanted me to leave my job? Did she know something I didn't about this position? *Whoa.*

No, I quickly thought, she knew exactly what she saw. She saw the light shining through me from my angels—facilitating my highest, best work. Dressing my soul in full regalia, my angels knew the pain I had experienced from the burning basement to the burning of the political war, the whole spectrum.

"Well, thank you, Bianca, I appreciate your courage to share your thoughts," I replied and left it there.

Bianca left my office. Her candor was a nudge. When my own assistant points out my highest work, I thought, I should listen.

The next day I wrote a brief letter to Phil McGraw of the *Dr. Phil* show, seeking financial support for OCBA and introducing our flagship program, Angel Faces. So many months went by without response that I forgot that I had written the letter. In the middle of the next retreat, my phone rang.

The girls were in a journaling assignment, so I took the call. For thirty minutes, I chatted with a man who identified himself as being with the Dr. Phil Foundation. He asked about the retreats, what I wanted for Angel Faces and myself. I assumed he was an intern working for the show and tried to let go of any expectations. As it was the middle of the retreat, I was fairly well fixated on pulling the girls through their healing.

Later that night I tossed in my bed thinking about the stories of pain and courage I'd heard that day. Restless, I popped open my laptop and googled the name of the man I'd spoken with earlier. My eyes blinked when I read he was the President and CEO of the Dr. Phil Foundation. At that point my insomnia became full bloom.

The retreat rolled to a close several days later. I never heard back from this gentleman with the Dr. Phil Foundation. Months passed.

Letting go is art. I'm no artist. I couldn't stop pondering what I had said to him. Did I speak too openly from the heart? Was the phone call a joke? What a skeptic! Such were my trust issues, a residual effect of my recent agony of betrayal, which I so desperately wanted to forget.

Bruce rode his motorcycle across the country in mid-August 2006 as part of a large 911-memorial ride. I flew into Pennsylvania where he saddled me on the back, and off we rode with a group of 3,500 motorcyclists, mostly police and firefighters from all over the United States, into New York City for 911's fifth anniversary.

It was a difficult decision not to ride my own Harley Davidson across country. Something inside of me changes when I ride into the wind. This decision to ride on the back of Bruce's proved to be a life changer given what call I received next.

A few days after the festivities we headed home to California on the motorcycle with a few other bikers. On an open road somewhere in Ohio, I felt my phone vibrating. At the next gas stop I looked at my phone—a missed call from a Los Angeles area code. I listened to the voicemail message.

"Hello, Lesia, this is Steve Davidson with the Dr. Phil Foundation. We spoke awhile back. Could you please call me? The message trailed off with the roar of the Harleys starting up.

"Come on, Babe, jump on … we're rolling," my husband Bruce signaled.

It would be another 150 miles until the next gas station. This gave me time to visualize what I wanted while trying to recall the conversation months ago.

Over the roar of the engines, I bellowed into Bruce's ear about the voice message I just received from the Dr. Phil Foundation and warned him that at the next stop I needed to make an important call. Our thoughts and the motorcycle raced over the next 150 miles.

At the next stop, I sprang off my seat and dashed off to a quiet place to return the call.

"Hello, Lesia, nice to hear from you," the gentleman answered. We exchanged niceties and I explained that I was on the back of my husband's Harley somewhere in the middle of Ohio heading back to California.

He asked for a formal proposal on Angel Faces for consideration, including a strategic plan and proposed budgets, the type of document that would take a talented committee a long time to prepare.

"Sure, I can get that to you," I replied. "When do you need it?"

"The sooner the better—next week?" he requested.

Holy moly! The motorcycles started to roar. Bruce's finger was in the air circling, his signal for me to get on. We were leaving. At times like these I wished men wore lipstick, or needed to fix their hair. An extra ten minutes would've helped me finish my call.

"I'll get a proposal to you in the next ten days," I told Mr. Davidson.

Back on the road in Ohio's green rolling hills, I realized that I had to catch a flight home from the next big city and write a proposal. Steve Davidson's call was my invitation to the change I suspected was coming.

"This is something big I should act on," I told Bruce, shouting into his ear. Over the roar and speed of the motorcycle, with the wind whipping into our faces, I continued, "I need to go home and write a proposal."

He was quiet for a moment, and then replied, "Cincinnati is 230 miles away. We'll be there in five hours. Let's discuss this at the hotel."

The next five hours of riding through beautiful countryside filled us both with the excitement of what was coming next.

I flew home to California from the Cincinnati airport the following morning with my husband's blessings and support, again. Bruce continued riding across the country with his friends while I sat at my small home office in California and pounded out a proposal for the future of Angel Faces, our future, the future of every adolescent girl with serious burn injuries or trauma who came to me. The proposal was on Mr. Davidson's desk by Friday.

The following day I caught a plane to Colorado to finish the ride home on the back of my husband's Harley, where I belonged.

As my passion for Angel Faces grew, my duties as the executive director at the Orange County Burn Association (OCBA) seemed increasingly stale. The long commute was becoming a drag; my dear friend and nurse manager, Victoria, had just retired; and Angel Faces was getting more attention.

Every time I did presentations to Orange County groups about OCBA and UCI programs and services, hands continuously went up with interest about Angel Faces. My guilt pangs increased. My annual contract was up for renewal in two months. What was I going to do?

Perhaps one of the gifts of surviving a trauma, war, or abandonment of any kind is isolation, *time alone.* Long hours alone in a hospital bed, in a battlefield where seconds seem like hours, at a prisoner of war camp, or other isolation venues anywhere provide an opportunity to trust yourself.

I knew that whatever happened in my life, whatever loss I had suffered, *I would never leave me.* I could always, no matter where I was, wrap my arms around me and soothe me into God's lap. Yet reality is there with decisions to make, actions to roll out. Besides, I couldn't spend my life standing around with my arms intertwined over myself, protecting me. I had long ago learned how to do that internally as I stood before anyone. I would never abandon myself. I had to live, and live fully.

Yet I continued to vacillate. I absolutely loved working so closely with the Burn Center at UCI. The burn team was my family. Dr. Marianne Cinat was a burn surgeon with amazingly healing bedside comfort. She cared about the whole patient. I respected her immensely. *Should I leave? If I don't now, then when?*

I sold some rental property Bruce and I had, so we had a little cash stashed in the bank to fall back on if I decided not to renew my contract.

The phone rang and my assistant Bianca answered. "Hold, please," I heard her say. She ran into my office, held her hands in prayer and said, "It's him, Mr. Davidson from the Dr. Phil Foundation.

I exhaled. A quick prayer shot from my lips and I picked up the phone.

"Hello, this is Lesia," I sang.

Mr. Davidson explained that he received my proposal and asked a lot more questions. He shared that they were considering doing a small piece about Angel Faces early the next year. That was four months away.

We talked about my position at OCBA, our program and services (besides Angel Faces) and our strong relationship with UCI Burn Center. I openly shared with him that I was thinking of leaving OCBA to grow Angel Faces but it would be so hard because of my commitment to the burn center and its patients.

"Well, Lesia … you are having a defining moment," Mr. Davidson stated.

I asked him if I left OCBA, was I giving, up the possible connection with The Dr. Phil Foundation?

"Lesia, we will follow you wherever you go," he said. "It's Angel Faces we're sort of interested in." He left me with no commitment, just inquiring interest.

I hung up the phone and looked at my calendar. My contract was up for renewal in thirty-two days. I felt I owed OCBA a thirty day notice. That left me two days to decide. I called my husband, who reiterated that he fully supported my decision to leave. He wanted me back home; the commute was hard on him too. His support helped me come alive, each cell in my body regenerating at high levels.

I made my decision. I was not going to renew my contract. I was going home.

I had to research the lengthy process for Angel Faces to get a 501c3 non profit status, recruit a board of directors, design a strategic plan, create budgets and recruit volunteers. Then there was the fundraising. I had a lot of work to do.

My plan was that after my last day at OCBA, October 31st, I would take November and December off, enjoy the holidays and think about how I wanted to structure Angel Faces. Besides, *The Dr. Phil Show* wasn't even interested maybe until early next year, if at all.

Then came the hardest part.

I began the short walk from my office across the street to the burn center. I owed it to Dr. Cinat to tell her in person that I was not renewing my contract and would be leaving in thirty days. As I stepped off the curb, I flashed back over the last three and half years that I had worked there. Even as Dr. Cinat treated the burn-injured, she and her staff had unknowingly healed my pain from UCSD and the Burn Institute fiasco.

With this profound gratitude in mind, I walked down the hall to a patient's room with Dr. Cinat. She stopped to look at me.

"Lesia, before you joined our burn team, it was as if I had a plant in my office that was dying, leaves wilting off and starving for love and attention. When you came on board with us, it is as if that same plant grew incredibly large leaves, emerald in color, strong and taller. One can't help but feel alive in your presence." She pressed on, "Lesia, that's what you have done for our burn team and our patients. We are so blessed to have you."

Now I was going to tell her that I was leaving? Good grief. I pushed through my discomfort. I had to.

"Dr. Cinat, I have some news for you," I gingerly shared.

"What is it, Lesia?" she asked.

"Dr. Cinat, I need to leave. I need to grow Angel Faces and I'm feeling like I'm not doing my highest and best work here …" I exhaled.

"Oh no, Lesia, this is not good for us—but I respect your decision." Dr. Cinat seemed annoyed. Deafening silence loomed between us.

I explained to her that when I was hired, I was on the path of launching Angel Faces as a non profit, but Victoria offered me the position and opportunity as an alternative. As I went on, Dr. Cinat took my news hard. She was supportive yet disappointed with traces of frustration.

"Oh, Lesia, what a loss for us and our patients! We have worked so hard together with the university bringing in our burn support programs to the patients. I'm so sad," she expressed. "We will really miss you." She was genuinely happy for me to be independent, but her baby was the burn center, its team, and patients.

I'm not sure what was worse—hearing the disappointment in her voice or the next morning standing with the team after rounds and sharing the news about my departure. It was bitter sweet.

The last few days of my position as executive director at OCBA, Dr. Phil's producer called to ask if I would be a guest on the show with a panel of women who were passionate about a cause.

"It would give you a brief opportunity to talk about Angel Faces," he offered. I agreed, thinking it was my only shot at promoting Angel Faces on *Dr. Phil.*

A camera crew arrived at our home. I did a sit-down interview in the living room and they shot various footages of me there. The producer spotted my collection of heart-shaped rocks and became excited. "Shoot this collection," he told the camera crew.

When I showed the producer my enormous shiny Harley Davidson, he asked if he could get footage of me riding. I put on my gear, including my pink helmet and roared up the street. It seemed like a lot of filming for a brief part on a panel of women. Well, a lot would be lost on the editing room floor.

In early November after I left OCBA, a producer from the *Dr. Phil show* abruptly announced to me over the phone that the panel was upcoming. They sent a car for me and my husband. We spent the night at a hotel in Hollywood and were picked up again the following morning and taken to Paramount Studios. As we entered through the gate my mind flashed to all the old Hollywood glamorous movie stars of the 1940s. I felt dreamy.

Bruce and I sat in the green room as the nervous energy of many producers and associate producers surged in and out.

I asked one of the producers, "I'd like to meet the other women who are sharing a panel with me. Don't we need to practice what we are to discuss?"

"Sorry, gotta get back on the set, Lesia. I'll be right back."

The more people I asked, the fewer visited us in the green room.

It was time. After I was miked up, they escorted Bruce and me out into the audience to seats right in front of the stage. It was a packed audience yet very quiet as we entered. My husband and I were the last to be seated.

"Can I get you anything?" the stagehand asked as he directed us to sit.

"Yes, I'd love some water," I replied, parched. He requested water for me through his earpiece and within a moment, water appeared with a straw so as to not smear my lipstick. This production was clearly professional.

"Watch that screen right there," he pointed to a large white panel. I nodded. I'd given up asking about the panel of experts I was to be a part of.

Dr. Phil and his wife Robin came onstage and *bam*, there it was, my entire life story depicted on the big screen. After the video was over, Dr. Phil walked up to me, extended his hand and helped me onstage. I was totally floored.

Through my shock and tears we talked about Angel Faces and my journey. He and Robin presented me with the "Heart of a Woman" award that they had only given to one other woman previously—that woman had swam the English Channel. This award came with a beautiful Tacori diamond heart-shaped necklace. It was now clear why they filmed the heart rocks in my house.

As if the award and diamond necklace were not enough, they presented me with a check for Angel Faces; $50,000 dollars from Mary Kay Cosmetics Foundation. My face was a fountain of tears.

As I gasped for composure, Dr. Phil next explained that one of my girls wanted to thank me in person for how I impacted her life.

Seeing Crystal walk across the stage broke me into a fresh episode of sobs. Her appearance was a miracle, though only I knew that at the time. The darling girl from my first Angel Faces retreat who had bolted out of the cafeteria at the sight of strangers had a crippling fear of crowds or going out in public with her scars. Here she was in front of millions of people and a live audience and now on the stage at the *Dr. Phil* show, walking towards me.

Yes, you have to be careful what you wish for, but you also have to be careful what you think of. Thoughts expand into behavior that leads to manifestation. Thought is a beautiful and powerful tool and needs to be used properly.

Obviously, the "panel of women" did not exist, though a panel of my angels giggled high above me. This day gave me the nod that I was on the right path.

It was a long quiet ride back to our home from the studio. Bruce and I both knew the path before us would be both challenging and rewarding—and definitely a lot of hard work.

CHAPTER TEN

Healing
Hearts

*Out stepped a few girls
covered in scars and carrying
their broken hearts.*

The unexpected $50,000 check from the Mary Kay Foundation, through the Dr. Phil Foundation, meant Angel Faces could launch independently. I raced to work immediately. My plan to have three months off was only a dream, a dream still waiting today.

I switched gears and jumped into filing for nonprofit status (which I had no idea how to do). I had to create an organizational development plan, and then design and recruit a new board of directors that could roll out a strategic purpose for Angel Faces' mission.

That begged the question ... what was our precise mission? Then there was the search for the right person to hire part-time, setting up my home office, and planning for the next retreat.

The work was mounting, pushing my skills and abilities to their maximum potential. Yet with my passion to heal, there was no stopping me.

The $50,000 check in hand, I walked into a large national bank, thinking I was now ready for the big time.

"I'd like to open up an account with a nonprofit status," I told the front person.

"Sure, have a seat, someone will be right with you," said a lady in a tight navy suit. Then she departed.

I sat in the uncomfortable chair and pondered. *Was this really happening?* My *Dr. Phil show* had not even aired yet and here I sat with a $50,000 check. It felt as if I had the world in my hand to create my dream. I began to sweat. How was I going to do all this ...

A man appeared in another ill fitted suit. "Hello, may I help you?"

"Yes, hello," I said standing. "I'd like to open an account." I followed him to his private desk.

"I need to open an account for my nonprofit," I said, excitedly.

"Where are your nonprofit papers, your 501c3 status papers?" he asked.

"They are still being processed. I just filed, but I have this check to deposit." I handed him the check. He stared at the check for a moment and left the office, saying, "I'll be right back."

Another uncomfortable chair, I thought. Well, I could open a checking account in my name, then when the papers arrived announcing my 501c3 status I could transfer the money. My mind was racing; I had so much to do.

The man returned, "I'm sorry, Mrs. Cartelli, we cannot accept this check into an account without a non profit status." I was a little surprised but understood that not providing forms was a momentary stumbling block—but he didn't offer any suggestions as to how I might proceed. Yet I'd thought of the simple solution in the minutes he was out of the office. He was certainly not resourceful (wasn't a bank all about customer service?) ... and where was the banker he ran this by? Did that mean two people at a national bank were leaving a prospective new business customer in the lurch holding a $50,000 check? Clearly, this was not the place for me. Who wants my money and to watch my dream blossom? Not this bank, apparently.

The next day I popped into my small credit union.

"Hello, Mrs. Cartelli, what can I do for you?" the familiar teller smiled at me.

"Hello ... Say, I have this check and I'd like to open up a nonprofit ... " I began.

Before I could finish, the bank manager approached me, "Hi there, Lesia, nice to see you. What can I do for you?" she asked.

Within fifteen minutes, the check was deposited in my new nonprofit-status account called "Angel Faces." Credit union staff ordered checks, and then politely put temporary checks in my hand. I was on my way with my to-do list— creating my dream.

In the swirl of setting up the framework of a nonprofit, I still had a retreat to plan. I was loving life—with the lawsuit behind me. Hearing my angels, I was moving on. Now to pull together an amazing team of volunteers!

At the retreat, my "High Tribe" of volunteer women was all on hand for the orientation, each of them exuding love and devotion. They sat amongst the girls with their spiritual gifts resting invisibly in their laps— waiting to share. How did I get so lucky? Their skills and vitality mean everything to the program. I glanced up to catch Jill's watery eyes.

Pure beauty is seeing someone willing to step into the arena of encouragement for a stranger. If our eyes are open, we see this love every day—strangers helping strangers, the wounded stretching their hearts to heal others' wounds.

Jill, a retired fire captain, had her own hidden trauma. She lost her husband Jimmy, also a firefighter, to a heart attack just weeks after he responded to the 911 tragedy in New York. He was only 47. I was buried deep in my own pain of the lawsuit when I heard of Jimmy's death. They had both volunteered as lifeguards at burn camp years before. Hearing that he'd died, I reached out to tell Jill that I was planting a beautiful white rose bush in Jimmy's honor.

Hadn't I learned that deep loss comes with tremendous gifts? Jill wasn't the kind of person who would want to waste her pain. I wanted Jill's energy to be a part of my team. Some time had now passed since Jimmy's death. It seemed safe to call upon her.

"Hi, Jill, it's Lesia. How are you, honey?"

"I'm OK, Lesia. It's nice to hear your voice," Jill replied.

"Jill, you may have heard that I launched a retreat for adolescent girls to help them heal from trauma and loss … I began to explain the program. As I took a breath, Jill spoke up.

"Lesia, I'm in! I've been wanting to be involved, waiting for you to ask me," she revealed.

Jill initially accepted our position as the retreat lifeguard but soon also stepped in to teach yoga to the participants and volunteers each morning. Yoga was an important vehicle in healing her grief. Now she was sharing the practice with us. Her leadership has always helped us remember to balance, breathe, and honor our bodies. When it's time for a swim, she protects the kids from water's dark side.

The retreats are often the first time the girls have donned a swimsuit since their accident. No public pool would feel emotionally safe, not with such horrific scars. Our pool is private and with our lifeguard protecting them, the girls have total freedom, to be just that … . girls.

Many other volunteer women are pillars holding Angel Faces up for the highest good of our girls we serve.

Kiyo is a vice president of a wealth management division of a large private banking institution, one of the wealthiest in our country. Her workday consists of donning pearls and heels while working closely with the most powerful and successful clients of our time. Kiyo has opportunities to be anywhere in the world, sailing in the Mediterranean or skiing in the Alps, yet she spends her time with us.

To witness someone taking a step forward in embracing tragedy, whether from a small accident, loss of a loved one or illness, is a remarkable gift. It is the human spirit wanting to grow, wanting to be free of pain and wanting to heal to a new level.

At the retreat she pulls on her shorts, slips into flip flops, and digs in, loving and caring for the girls beyond measure. She is our dorm mom. She washes the hair of those who have no fingers; rubs moisturizer on their dried, scared, mottled scars; ties their shoe laces; brushes and fixes their hair—doing all she can to get them to each session on time to nurture their wounded souls.

Heat is crippling for anyone with severe burns. Often Kiyo drags fans into their rooms and lugs out dirty laundry to the washer. This is Kiyo's other side—a woman of heart-driven service, full of love and grace for the girls.

Piper is another steady pillar for Angel Faces. A fire captain with eyes that have seen too much in our rescue world. Piper chooses to step away from what pleasures her in her off time (adventure travel), and volunteers with us to cradle the program into success. She organizes logistics with a watchful eye on safety measures. Piper is the glue of our operations. Its Piper's eyes I search for when challenged during the retreat.

A few years ago Piper was diagnosed with breast cancer. During the retreat, she commuted daily (two hours round-trip) for radiation treatments after months of enduring chemotherapy. She wanted to be with us, needed us, needed us to need her. Piper is a thread woven into our strong family. Together we're creating a blanket of healing.

I've witnessed again that healing happens on both sides, to those we serve—the girls—and to us *when* we serve.

Like an expectant mother, I knew the retreat was coming. I could feel the swell of emotion with each new blessing. My heart was the fullest when new girls found us, needing us, needing the soft place to fall that I was determined to deliver.

My phone rang early one morning. Nancy, a corrective cosmetic professional who volunteered with us, was calling from the Midwest. She blurted through the phone, "Lesia … I have a girl who needs Angel Faces. She's 16, a runway career model type. Stunningly gorgeous, she's got … well, *had* everything going for her until a horrific accident in her chemistry class."

Oh! I thought. These defeatist conclusions are everywhere, a worse enemy than the accidents. I caught my breath, then blurted, "Nancy, you mean she *does* have everything going for her and now more … we know somewhere in our heart that suffering a tragedy is a gift—and with time she will see the gift." Unrelenting, I seemed not to miss a beat. Perhaps my angels were speaking through me.

"Oh, Lesia, I love you. Thanks for reminding me. I forgot who I was talking to."

"So what happened to her?" I asked.

My heart sank as the story unfolded. Calais was in a chemistry class in a small private school in Ohio. Her teacher was conducting a class experiment, which called for lighting various explosive liquids to demonstrate flame color. Calais, being a brilliant and inquisitive student, was closest to the experiment with notepad in hand. An open flame was involved, and a large explosion occurred.

Our journeys are so personal, yet we grasp for hope when we need it. Living as an example of strength and courage is more powerful than any words.

Not only was Calais at an unbearable age to lose her *physical* beauty but her mother owned a modeling agency, a business promoting a belief system that centers on physical beauty. Calais's abrupt change of life-as-she-knew-it was made even harder by the fact that her family was devastated.

"I don't know if I can get her to the retreat, but I'm going to work on it. That's my goal." I could hear the passion and determination in Nancy's voice.

In weekly messages updating me on Calais's condition and her tumbling depression, Nancy's hope of convincing Calais to attend the retreat sank.

"I talked to her mom," Nancy reported on one of the more hopeful days. "She really wants her daughter to go and, of course, feels she needs it."

It wasn't as if I hadn't "been there" myself like Calais, but at that moment I was so filled with the light that was shining on Angel Faces and on me, I was able to say: "Well, Nancy, we do our best and then we must surrender and let our angels guide the girls to us. If she is meant to be with us, she will come."

Two weeks before the retreat my phone rang. Before I could say hello, Nancy squealed into the phone, "She's coming! Calais is coming with me to the retreat!"

I first saw Calais when she and Nancy stood on the curb at the San Diego Airport. Nancy waved her arm in the air, flagging me down.

I popped out and gave Nancy a massive hug and then looked over Nancy's shoulder at Calais. Beyond Calais's defensive social armor, I saw a beautiful, statuesque young lady. She flashed her eyes up at me then dropped them quickly. Her shoulders were all but pinned together in front. She was trying to protect her heart and cover the burn scars crawling over her body, everywhere.

I clasped her hands together in between us. "So lovely to meet you, Calais. Welcome to beautiful San Diego!" I squealed. Calais reciprocated with a warm yet nervous smile. We loaded the luggage, and I ran around the vehicle to the driver side.

"Hop in, ladies," I sang. Calais edged into the back seat; I could feel her eyes piercing through the back of my head.

During breakfast at a small cafe in my hometown, Encinitas, patrons stared at Calais. This was hard for me to see, yet I wondered whether they were staring at her horrific scars or her immense beauty. Was it beauty only I could see?

Being that this was my favorite local joint for lattes and muffins, I wondered if people stared at me when I was here without makeup. Maybe I had stopped noticing over the years, until then.

I kicked into maximum awareness, focusing on how Calais reacted to the people around us. I didn't want to stare at her posture, her body language, yet it was obvious by how protectively she held herself that she needed Angel Faces.

Gifts come to all of us. If you breathe, you have gifts. It takes courage to uncover them, recognize them and share your gift to the world, for the world's highest good.

Back at my house I watched Calais take in the setting I share with Bruce. Normalcy, not victimhood, was around her. I watched her shoulders begin to relax. I felt, or hoped I felt, her heart lifting and thought, *oh, good—and we haven't even gotten to the retreat yet.*

Nancy kept nudging me throughout the morning whispering, "Lesia, this is so great. I'm actually seeing her open up like a flower." I smiled. We were just getting started.

"So when did you get married?" Calais asked as she stared at our wedding picture.

"Not until I was 36-years-old, so seven years ago," I answered, intuiting that the question issued from her fear of never being loved.

"Where did you meet him?" She was curious, but the scars so prevalent on her face and body like mine were obviously on her mind.

"Oh, at a conference," I smiled. "That is a long story for another time." I wanted to keep the focus on her.

"I doubt I will ever meet a man who will love me because of how I look," Calais lowered her head.

"Give yourself time, Calais, and be easy with yourself. You have an extraordinary journey ahead of you that will require all of your brilliance, strength, and courage," I replied. I walked outside, not wanting to push her.

At my house, Nancy spent time teaching Calais how to apply corrective cosmetics while I subtly coached Calais to move beyond her injury to embrace life, ever so gently.

We continued our preparations, enmeshed in last minute *boots on the ground* work that always happens prior to a retreat. Calais sat on the floor sorting out bags of products—corrective cosmetics and skin care.

"Lesia, this is a lot of work!" Calais blurted out. "At the retreat, if any of the girls complain about even the littlest thing, I'm going to tell them how much work and passion went into creating it."

Nancy and I chuckled at her innocence. Opening boxes from sponsors and discovering what they'd sent for correcting scars was the fun part. These three days of toil were nothing compared to the preparation we started the year before. Add to that the decades that had passed since I crawled from the burning basement.

On the first day of the retreat my team and I stood at the front entrance waiting for the girls. I truly saw us as angels—wings sweeping a swath strong and wide—waiting for the wounded souls—more angels!—to appear. All but trumpets bellowed from the heavens.

We'd set up registration under the pop-up tent, where forms lay anchored by rocks in the breeze. Snacks were being prepared in the kitchen. The girls would be hungry after traveling great distances. Yes, hungry and not just for food. And just like other retreats, it would take until midweek to get a decent gauge of their deepest hunger and see how the program fed their soul.

The first van appeared. Out stepped a few girls covered in scars and carrying their broken hearts. I could feel my own heart start to weep for them. I'm not in control of this retreat, I had to keep telling myself. *This is God's work. Stand up tall, Lesia, I heard His whisper, you and your team have been called to duty.*

I am always eager to embrace the girls, particularly the first time. For me, the hardest yet greatest moment of the retreats comes when the van doors open. Until this point, I only know each of them as a name, a story, and a picture. Then I glimpse at the pain, the hurt and the hunger in person. The full depth of our ambition for these girls hits me. It's very humbling, and experience has taught me that our love, wisdom and answers will help all that gnaws at them.

Why me? I often hear from them. Why not you? I reply.

Traveling across the country requires enormous bravery from them. They must leave their nest and face public scrutiny at airports or train stations, and finally a cast of strangers at the retreat site itself. Their hope for a better life drives them to us. This is why I was burned, I remind myself every time. This is my gift, to serve.

Getting the girls settled was a bit awkward. It always is. As my volunteers took the teenagers to their rooms, they stole glances at each other. Like before, we'd chosen a beautiful, healing venue—their new home for the coming week. I wondered if they'd all end up in the same room that night, sleeping foot to face, like at the first retreat—just wanting to feel included. I hope so, I whispered to myself.

After unpacking, the girls came to the guesthouse for our first gathering of introductions and orientation. This would be the second hardest moment for me. I opened the program with a ritual ringing of the chimes, a spiritual welcome, followed by soft introductions. I fought back burning tears. Our frivolous icebreakers glossed over the pain of why they were there, but they had to be done.

Each girl shared their name, where they were from, and something "fun" about themselves. Once back in their place, the orientation continued. I could see their hungry, wounded eyes penetrating me for answers. Their expressions were almost too tender to be endured. Hadn't I been there so many years ago, walking into my fourth grade class horribly scarred?

Now I stood here at the head of a program I had created from my own pain. By the time of this first retreat under our own independent nonprofit status, I had done this already several times, each retreat took my hard work, careful planning, concentrated attention, and—most of all—listening to God and my angels. I knew that fear or failure or rejection would be fruitless and maybe even destructive.

I kept telling myself: *We are home. They are home.*

On the second day at our "grief and loss" session, girls could voluntarily share their story. Amazingly, many of them had never had this opportunity before. (This is often the case.) In solidarity, we witnessed them breaking open. I write "breaking," because it can be very traumatic to let go when you've been stuffing your feelings for a long time. How well I knew! "Opening" to allow the darkness to depart is never easy, but it's often the only way to let light enter.

Don't be afraid to pull the covers off someone who is hurting—allowing their light to shine.

As girls began to share their stories, we listened to them relay the horrific details in quavering voices. Yesnaya, age sixteen, sat next to me on the floor. She came to us from Cuba. A seemingly tough girl, her alpha energy and bold voice were there to defend the heavy scars draped over her face.

I could feel Yesnaya's pain as she sat right next to me. The boisterous shell that protected her deep pain seemed to crack with each new story shared. Silence filled the room as each girl gathered courage to share their story. I looked next to me and gently nodded at Yesnaya, "Are you ready to share?" I whispered.

"Well, when I was three-years-old, I got burned in Cuba. I was home ... something caught fire ..." she said sniffling. At the time my mother was pregnant with my little sister. My little sister, you see ... something is wrong with her now. It's her brain. She just ain't right." Yesnaya fought back tears, lowered her head, in a quiet voice.

"You see, my mama was so stressed and worried about me being all burnt up and trying to always get to the hospital to be with me ... I think that's why my little sister was born with medical problems. It's all my fault." Now a tear rolled down her cheek.

We sat in silence, holding space for Yesnaya to say, everything she needed to say. Nothing more left her lips. I turned to her sending love and compassion through my eyes. She was done sharing, but something told me that wasn't the end of it.

The next day was the "butterfly release" ceremony. We have real butterflies (still asleep in cocoon-like folded paper) shipped to the facility. Midweek we gather on the yoga field at dusk with prayer and intention to release our hurt and pain. Each girl receives an envelope holding a butterfly ready to unfold. As the invocation finishes, the girls release both their butterflies and their pain. It's always a beautiful experience. The butterflies soar overhead. The music closes the ritual.

As I walked to the edge of the field that day, I could feel a hand pulling on the back of my shirt. I turned back.

"Oh, Yesnaya! Hey, baby ... wasn't that beautiful—seeing the butterflies taking our pain away?"

"Yeah ..." she whispered.

Suddenly, she threw her arms around me and sobbed. I stood firm and held her while she cried hard for what seemed an eternity. Everyone had left the field except our amazing therapist Carol, who had somehow sensed "growth" about to happen.

Carol was always present to cradle, coach, and support the girls. Meanwhile other girls waited for me nearby where the next program was scheduled to start. How do you pry a teenager buried in tears and pain off your chest? But over Yesnaya's shoulder, there was Carol waiting with open arms.

"Yesnaya, baby girl," I whispered in her ear. "I'm giving you to Carol who can love and cradle you through this, OK? We are here, Yesnaya, here for you. And Carol ... well, you'll see. She knows exactly what to do." Yesnaya never spoke, just sobbed uncontrollably.

Yesnaya shifted to Carol's arms. Holding her tightly, Carol whispered, "Yesnaya, Honey, use your words and tell me what your tears are saying to you." Spoken like the awesome therapist she was, I nodded and shuffled off other waiting girls.

"This is the best experience of my life," I heard Yesnaya mumble on Carol's shoulder.

This is the best place God has placed me, I whispered up to the orange sky.

Yesnaya wept for hours that night. The next morning, I saw her at yoga. She looked different. Her inner light was brightly shinning.

"Good morning, Miss Lesia." She gave me a big smile as I walked up to her with my mat under my arm.

"My stars, it's nice to meet the new you, Yesnaya! You must've allowed last night's tears to cleanse you. Why, I can see your self-love. I'm so proud of you."

Yesnaya, nodded, "Me too, Miss Lesia. I feel better than I have ever felt in my life." Yesnaya went home after the retreat, cut her hair in a chic style, posted a picture online and claimed: *My life is changed for the better, forever.*

Yesnaya's experience of feeling responsible took me back to one of the early burn camps. There had been a little boy weeping at night, crying that he had to go home. Homesickness often sets in but this boy, whose name was Jose, was adamant that he needed to go home right away.

Surrendering to tears takes courage, whether you are sixteen-years-old or ancient. Cleansing a path to your tomorrow may require washing away your agony. Yet as it leaves for good, the weight uncovers light within you. For the first time your pain may be as light as a butterfly.

"Jose, why do you need to go home?" Bob, a firefighter who volunteered at the camp, had asked.

"My mom is pregnant."

"Oh, Jose, she will be fine," Bob reassured him, thinking that the accident had left Jose with anxiety about everything, also very common.

"No, I have to go home. I have to be there when she has the baby!" Jose's tears rolled over his scarred and mutilated face.

"Jose, she'll be fine. There are good doctors that will take care of her," Bob continued to nurture.

"No, you don't understand," Jose pleaded. "I must be there when she has the baby, because when she sees the baby isn't burned like me, she will love the baby more than me, and I have to make sure that doesn't happen." Jose continued to weep.

I got up and walked away from the conversation, with my heart too open to cope. Though the children's individuality gives each retreat its challenges and indeed its glory, these injured kids need so much love. And they *have* so much love to give.

CHAPTER ELEVEN

Watching Courage

*When we speak real truth,
its best we're prepared for
real truth returning.*

Haley, age 13, had maneuvered into the doorway sideways with protruding casts on both arms. Stiff, scared and locked in two widespread winged splints—a position no thirteen-year-old blonde, blue-eyed girl should ever be in.

"Welcome ... you must be Haley," said Diane, who was greeting enrollees at the registration table.

"Um, hi," Haley responded as she shuffled up to the table.

"You've come so far, all the way from Texas," Diane beamed.

"Um ... yeah, um ... " Haley was exhausted yet tried to be friendly.

Haley was the most recently burned participant at the retreat. Burned over sixty percent of her upper body just four months prior in yet another school science project gone awry, she was bandaged from her neck to her knees. She needed bandages on her face too, but air-travel security frowns on covered faces.

All week Haley sat quietly on the couch during our sessions.

Concerned about her, I had several nights of tossing and turning. "Is she understanding our teachings?" I asked my tribe of volunteers. They tried to be positive, but they couldn't get a read on Haley either. After seven days, Haley's family came to pick her up. Three family members pushed through the door, and her mother Joni's eyes filled with tears when she saw Haley.

Once home, Joni called to exclaim, "Lesia, as soon I walked in the door to pick Haley up I saw the light in her eyes. I knew I got my Haley back!" Haley went home to embark on a long road of more reconstruction surgery. I worried about her. It's the quiet ones who are most vulnerable.

You can imagine my fear when just months after the retreat Haley was headed back to school. Even with my own school experiences decades behind me, I remained petrified for "my girls." With school, come horrific challenges in trying to fit in when one looks so 'different'; especially when accidents are school related.

Yet months after starting school Haley mustered the courage to ask the cutest boy in her high school to take her to the school prom. Haley wore a black halter dress and red corsage over her marbled, scared body. This retreat of healing doesn't happen alone, it takes enormous devotion from big hearts.

Gathering the needed volunteers to make Angel Faces a success year after year was divinely driven. I didn't want just warm bodies. They were everywhere. I needed strong, professional, centered, self-aware and most importantly *fun*-to-be-with women. God delivered people like Jill and others in unusual ways.

Each year my husband Bruce and I host a Christmas party, inviting mostly fire department folks and their spouses. Around the time that we were strengthening the Angel Faces dream, in walked Diane and Ken. I knew Ken as a battalion chief with the Oceanside Fire Department. He had also volunteered in the ropes course during my burn-camp leadership.

When I volunteered as a family support liaison for San Diego's Urban Search and Rescue team that was deployed to the 911 tragedy, I met his wife Diane. Diane was a fire captain in a ferocious small town east of Los Angeles. She met all my volunteer requirements perfectly, especially the fun part.

"What did you do to your wrist?" I pointed to the cast on her hand.

"Oh, I fell down a children's slide at a funeral," she grinned.

I couldn't walk away from subject matter this tantalizing.

"Oh, do tell," I asked.

"A dear friend recently died of brain cancer. The funeral was at her home. I saw her grandson moping about the solemn crowd and thought I could distract him with a bit of boyish fun. So I hiked up my skirt to chase him up a four-foot slide. Obviously, I had outgrown the moment. I lost my footing and extended my right hand to break my fall, breaking my wrist in several places." Diane held a glass of wine in one hand, cradling the cast.

Like I mentioned early in the book—angels come in every form and they are everywhere! Stay open and stay grateful, even in the simplest of encounters.

"Whoa, how can you fight fire in a cast?" I inquired.

"I can't. I'm off duty to heal but I'm keeping busy making beautiful jewelry. It's good for physical therapy."

There before me were the makings of a gifted Angel Faces volunteer! Diane had turned her setback to a plus, and she was giddy about it.

"Oh, you make *jewelry*, Diane? I have just launched a unique retreat … perhaps you'd like to volunteer and help the girls make jewelry?" Having headed down this path, I then moved to seal the deal.

Diane was perfect—a firefighter with compassion for people with burn injuries who found humor in the simplest of tasks. She stepped in to create amazing art therapy projects with Angel Faces, a role that would evolve over the years. Each retreat carries a "theme," to which Diane matches the art project.

For instance, for a "let your light shine" retreat, the project was clear bottles drilled with holes, and threaded to the top with twinkle lights, anchored by a crystal. The girls spent time painting the bottles with the colors of how they wanted their light to shine. Once home, they plugged them in—reminders of the light within them.

In another example, the girls wove copper wire around a heart frame (made by Diane's husband Ken). The girls stuffed colored broken glass between the wires. These artifacts reminded them, "Although we have broken pieces in our hearts, our hearts are still beautiful—the sum of colored glass shining through." For nine years, Diane has led these art projects. A gift from breaking her wrist and the courage to not waste her pain!

• • •

The need for forgiveness weaves a strong cord through us all at the retreat. In my own heart, in the heart of the girls, in every heart, the issue of guilt is there to be addressed. Whether we need to forgive ourselves or others, or help others forgive themselves, forgiveness is a hard lesson for anyone to grasp, particularly when you are the one left disfigured.

"Girls, do you understand that not forgiving someone is like drinking poison every day and waiting for the other person to die?" I shared. I see them grab at the pen and journal, writing.

Some girls arrive at the retreats filled with anger. Bridgette was severely burned at the age of three. Her father was 'cooking' methamphetamine in the garage. Bridgette, an innocent babe, wandered into the garage to be with her daddy. Something went terribly wrong and the garage exploded, leaving Bridgette bald and severely scared, with slits for eyes.

At seventeen Bridgette was angry, rightly so. Nevertheless, I tried to show Bridgette that by not forgiving her father, she holds herself a prisoner. She remained shut away from life's blessings. Maybe holding onto that anger protected her, reminded her not to trust freely. But it also separated her from life's richness.

Opportunities to open your heart to signs of love on a daily basis will come to you in the meekest form. Someone holds a door open for you, shares his or her umbrella, lets you step in front of them in line. None of this can happen when you are stuck in anger. If it's too much to tackle on a daily basis, try forgiving for an hour, even a moment. Introduce yourself to what your life could be like by living in love.

Another type of forgiveness is the healing power of releasing someone else from guilt.

"My dad feels guilty," said Tiffany, age 16. "He told me the accident was his fault. But it really wasn't his fault. He just told me to keep the fire going while he went out to the field to get more corn to burn. It was what we always did together. After he left, there was a backdraft that came down the chimney as I was spraying the accelerant. I felt a breeze and then the fire came at me. I was the one who poured the accelerant on it. But, he still feels so bad. I can just tell." With Tiffany revealing this, I saw several other girls nod.

"Tiffany, have you talked to your father about how it wasn't his fault?" I asked.

Tiffany shook her head no. "I can't really talk to my dad. He's a strong farmer-type dad who never shows his feelings." I was stumped.

"Tiffany, how about writing him a letter? You can take your time composing it. When the right moment comes, you can hand it to him, avoiding all the emotion. He can read it in private on his own time."

"Well, I could try," she said sounding hesitant.

"Take your time writing it, Tiffany. It might take you weeks to write it, but it will be healing for both of you. You can always read it to me or someone else after it's written to see if you really want to give it to him," I offered.

Our session was over and the girls had left to enjoy an hour of free time. Our nurse Mary and I were meeting in the guesthouse when Tiffany sauntered in.

"Well … " she smiled at us.

"Well what? Tiffany, you OK?" Mary asked.

"Yes, I finished the letter and want you to read it." She handed me the letter.

"My stars, Tiffany, that was quick!"

I handed the letter back to her. "Baby, you wrote it. Read it to us from your heart," I suggested.

Tiffany read the letter. It was filled with wanting him to understand that he was not responsible, she didn't blame him and he needed to stop blaming himself. Her hand-written letter was two pages long with love dripping off the lines. I was impressed and deeply moved.

Mary and I stood with tears in our eyes, knowing this was a precious moment to be savored. If she really had the courage to give this to her father, it could be a turning point in the family's healing.

A week after the retreat my phone rang.

"Hello?" I answered.

"Hello, Lesia, it's Tiffany. I think it's time to give the letter to my dad."

"How are you going to do it?" I asked.

"I don't know. That's why I'm calling. He goes to bed really early. I'm thinking I'll put it on his pillow, and then he can read it alone cause my mom stays up late."

"Excellent plan. Just be sure to turn a light on so he sees it. And Tiffany, I'm so proud of you."

"Thank you. I'm scared but excited," she whispered.

"Scared is good. It means you're alive," I whispered back. Right then I was experiencing her nervous energy and anxious for the positive outcome I prayed the letter would bring.

Days went by and I called to follow up.

"Hello, it's Lesia. Well, how did it go? Did you leave the letter on his pillow?" I pried. I could feel her smiling through the phone line.

"Yes, I left it on his pillow and waited. Peeking through the door, I saw him read it. Moments later he came back out, crying, and gave me the biggest hug ever. I told him that I didn't blame him and that I was happy it was me instead of him." She went on.

"Lesia, before the letter, I felt like he couldn't even look at me. He just felt so bad and there was a clear wall between the two of us. The breakthrough we had was huge for everyone. Once he knew I was OK, he was OK, which made my mom and sister so happy."

I left the conversation knowing how hard it was for Tiffany to write that letter to her father. What a risk it was to open herself up and to receive emotions from people who are not good at sharing. Risky, yes, but well worth the risk. How many times have I chosen not to write a letter about things in my own heart? I hung up the phone in awe of her courage.

When we speak the truth from our heart about real stuff, baring real emotions, we best be prepared to get the real stuff back. That's good news. That's love. When given, we get it right back. Yet when we give anger, we'll get that back too.

• • •

Powerful transitions happen at the retreats. But they are not without challenges. There is the camera that went missing from one of our girls, then appeared under another girl's bed when we threatened to go through everyone's luggage.

Then there's the girl who was angry that I didn't assign her cousin as her roommate. "But you can't grow if you are glued together," I explained. All I got back from her were sour looks until the following year, when she sent in her application and wrote, "I loved the retreat. I must come back."

And the girl who was caught in the facility's kitchen using a volunteer's cell phone to call a boy whom she had met a week prior. This girl had already caused a lot of problems, which robbed the volunteers and other girls of our energy. We made the decision to send her home.

We called her parents, who were local, to come pick her up. Their reply was telling in and of itself: "We're at Six Flags Magic Mountain and we can't pick her up until 8 p.m. when the park closes." For seven hours, my team of volunteers took turns watching her sequestered in a room—forestalling her threats of running away.

We made a second decision to send another girl home midweek, because her anger issues were coming from her horrible home life. Her trauma was secondary. She wasn't interested in healing her pain. She was also depriving the other girls of the sacredness of our retreat environment.

The struggles that we face at the retreats come with pushing through our pain, their pain. These struggles build us all up to a stronger platform, strengthen us as a team, force us to press deeper and uncover our desire to find purpose, sometimes just for the day, hopefully for life. It often doesn't seem like an epiphany is happening when we're in the middle of the struggle, but we trust that it is happening.

• • •

I saw Mariah walk up the hill to registration with her family in tow after a long ride in the car from Colorado. Her hair was combed down, hiding almost half her face. Mariah, then thirteen, was born with no right eye or socket and a major cleft lip and palate anomaly. She had already endured twenty-eight surgeries where surgeons created an eye socket and inserted a blue glass eye to match her own. Yet after reading her application I was struck by her wish: she wanted to know what it was like to see out of both eyes.

Mariah also wrote in her application that she wanted to become a researcher to find a solution to her condition. I knew she was special. They are all special.

The first night I showed the girls the movie *Penelope*, starring Reese Witherspoon. It is about a girl born with an upturned nose that resembles a pig's nose. The premise is Penelope's journey of self-discovery. She decides to join a newfound friend on this ultimate journey whereby she accepts how she looks and shows the world she is all right. The movie ends with a man falling in love with her, cancelling the curse of the swine nose.

The time was ripe. On the last day hair stylists come to the retreat to help the girls break out of another shield they often hide behind—their hair. Mariah sat in the chair while Erin, a volunteer stylist, began to style her hair.

"So, Mariah, how are you going to change your hair?" I asked.

"Well, I'm just getting a little trimmed off the length in back," she replied in her signature soft voice.

"What about bangs? Maybe you should have Erin cut bangs to show the world your pretty eyes." I took a risk.

"No, that's OK. I'm just going to get a trim," she repeated, head down.

Silently crushed, I walked away, giving us both space. *C'mon God, you want me to do this type of work, You have to help me,* I whispered. A few minutes later I tried again.

"Still going to just get a trim, Mariah?" I gently pushed.

"Yeah," she flashed her one blinking eye at me.

I launched. "Mariah, honey, think about Penelope. You remember when her scarf fell off and she showed the world that she accepted how she looked different, finding beauty inside herself? And remember how the world responded with acceptance when she did and she began to really enjoy her life!?" I was pleading inside for God to help me with the right words.

"Yeah," Mariah looked up.

"Well …" I became silent. Mariah looked back at Erin holding the scissors.

"Erin, can you please give me bangs? I don't want to hide anymore." Mariah's voice lifted those words.

As it turned out, this moment was a turning point in Mariah's life. She went home a new person, embracing life. She even joined an Irish dance group where she dances competently with her head held high sporting bangs for the world to see.

• • •

The component of "our looks" gnaws away at everyone and for no one more than burn-damaged teenage girls. For the girls at the retreat, we address the topic of appearance in the corrective cosmetic room. Each girl receives one-on-one instruction with an array of various corrective cosmetics to try in private.

Her response to this therapy is a direct reflection of what's going on inside.

Courtney was burned in an accident at home. She is of African-American descent. Her injured dark complexion tended to produce keloid (raised up) scarring. She also has the challenge of hyper pigmentation and hypo pigmentation (which is uneven color, either too little melanin or too much). Courtney was sassy.

Her behavior was warm but very strong, in that she seemed to handle anything even though she had massive, thick scars crawling over her beautiful body. I walked into the corrective cosmetic room as Nancy was finishing her final touches on Courtney's face and legs, blending her tones—a true camouflage.

I was shocked to see how well the corrective cosmetic makeup minimized her scars. This would ward off a few more stares and questions from the public. Nancy held up the mirror to her as I entered. Courtney dropped her head in her hands and wept.

"Courtney, why are you crying?" I asked.

"Oh, Miss Lesia, I never thought I would ever look nearly normal again, until now." Courtney wiped her tears away.

"Hey, hey," Nancy jumped in. "Be careful, Courtney. Don't mess up your makeup!" she blurted mixed with her distinctive laugh.

As a teenage girl, when everyone was wearing makeup, I used to stand around the corner at a department store makeup-counter wishing I weren't burned, wishing I could step right up to the counter and experiment like the other girls. Over the years at the retreats, corrective cosmetic sessions are important to draw that eyebrow back on that was once burned off, or to tone down angry red scars.

Yet makeup is still just one aspect of renewing our relationship with our bodies. Most people—not just those who are physically wounded—move through life warily. Our bodies speak before our lips move. Evidence of this presents itself to us daily.

Notice the next time two people approach each other or when the conversation turns a little uncomfortable. Arms get crossed. Legs shuffle. Heads sink. Reading these signals, it appears that most everyone fundamentally bounces between protective mode and bravado!

Like clockwork, the girls at the retreat draw back when I explain about their scheduled massages and facials. Building therapeutic touch into the program helps them learn about the power of healing touch.

After a trauma, often patients are only touched by medical professionals and likely in a cold clinical setting.

Sadly, these encounters usually involve pain—dressing changes, staples removed, or donor-site cleaned. Being touched in a loving way is crucial to healing! And the touch needs to occur without the expectation of sex, guilt or the wow factor of someone wanting to experience thick, scarred skin.

As I went over the schedules for the following day, a thirteen-year-old named Tracy, who was badly burned in a house fire at the age of two, raised her hand and asked if the therapeutic-touch day was optional. She wore a wig to hide her hairless head. I could feel her angst from the front of the room. I conveyed, massages and facials were optional. With that I could see half the room release their shoulders.

Allowing someone to touch your damaged, disfigured body is difficult. I knew this. I once was terrified to get a massage for fear of the questions, quiet gasps when the sheet was pulled back. Today, I can't get enough of the kneading, open and yearning for healing hands.

Meeting her resistance, I called upon Tracy to be my model for the demonstration of what they were to expect in their massage session. Tracy climbed on the table, holding her wig. As my demonstration got underway, I kept my heart open for God to work through my hands to calm Tracy, while my mind stayed in teaching mode. After the demonstration was over, Tracy sat up and looked at me and asked, "Can I get back on the schedule?"

Training the masseuses at the spa reminded me that the soul is forever trying to heal. I stood in front of fourteen massage therapists preparing them to operate from their highest spiritual place when they work on our girls. Reminding them to protect their energy for if they open up completely to give the loving touch to the girls, the girls' trauma will slay them.

Deep pain resides in the cells of our body. We can love. We can touch. But we must protect ourselves. The goal is to find the balance between loving and protecting.

After the girls come out of their dimmed, lavender scented massage rooms, I feel and see the shift in their healing—the light shining through their once dim eyes, soft authentic smiles replace their nervous, *I'm fine* pursed grin. And at this moment, my team and I are blessed to witness their shift into self-love.

Still, though, I've learned—and they have, too—that some healing is only skin-deep. We can diminish our scarring with makeup, but our emotional pain can't be covered. Not really. "Stuffing" pain turns into disease, or "dis-ease," trapping it in a place where it cannot heal. The trapped pain then spills over into anger, depression, and other self-destructive behaviors.

When overcoming a trauma or serious injury, using attention from boys and men is another form of self-validation that though potentially enhancing doesn't fix anything deeply. Like corrective cosmetics and massage, romantic attentions are ego boosting, but ultimately only superficial additions in the tool box of acceptance and healing.

Whether it is the full corrective array or something as simple as lip-gloss, one date or many, making the effort says: "I'm worth it and I care about me." Or worse, I've seen girls want a baby, and have a baby for the wrong reason. They feel a baby in their arms shows the world that a boy 'cared' about them enough to have sex. This breaks my heart. I see it too often. External products and external relationships are only *one* tool to help on our healing path.

For true healing, we must confront the trauma deep within, then embrace it. When we clean up the darkness and pain within us, the corrective measure (whatever it is) allows the light within us to shine through.

Try this: Hold your chest out. Allow your shoulders to pull back to enfold an invisible golden cord of strength that is tethered from your spine to a source of something more powerful than you. Break open your heart, allowing the light to enter to what is real for you, what is true for you. Do this while breathing deeply.

Do you feel the difference? It's your acceptance of an invitation to an enriched journey. A start.

CHAPTER TWELVE

Bouquet of Many Layers

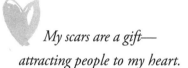

*My scars are a gift—
attracting people to my heart.*

Judgment is human nature, with visual impressions being perhaps our strongest invitation to judgment. The perception of how others look and how we look dictates our thoughts and our thoughts turn to action. It's the judgment of ourselves and others that can either keep us stuck or move us forward.

If my face were without trauma, or if the scars that crawled over my body were gone, who would I be? For so long

I pretended they weren't there. It was my coping mechanism. It worked for awhile, got me through school.

Finally, I realized that what I was really doing was teaching people to treat me as I though I looked normal. Was I lying to myself? Probably. The reality is I didn't look normal. It wasn't until my first burn camp at Lake Tahoe that this reality and my trauma came bubbling up—bubbling up ... to heal.

Early in my relationship with Bruce, while we were still dating, I shared a large home in Encinitas, California, with four other young women. We were all in our late twenties, early thirties. My four roomies were your typical southern California girls. They owned their natural beauty; they were athletic and healthy. We were all single. You can imagine the swinging front door of dates they attracted. Equally handsome young men, searching for a "hot" girl, could be certain that at least one of my roommates would fill the bill.

Late one Friday night I was standing in the kitchen munching on a snack and the front door whirled opened and then slammed shut. Sarah, the youngest of my roomies, was dressed attractively and classy for a typical date night. She stormed into the kitchen, tossing her handbag on the counter, clearly upset.

"Hey, so how was the date?" I smiled though I could tell by her expression that it didn't go well.

"Whoa, Lesia, don't you hate it when you go on a date with a guy and he wants you to wear a skirt up to here?" With that her hand slammed against her mid-thigh. "Or your boobs to hang out to here and high heels to the heavens?" Sarah blurted out.

"No, I have no clue what you are talking about," I shared as I munched away.

"WHAT!? Yes, you do! You've been out with guys that do that! Everybody has," she replied.

"No … not me, Sarah. Guys who want a girl to look like *that* are not interested in me," I said.

"Seriously? she said.

"Seriously," I confirmed.

"Oh, man, do you see how lucky you are? Your scars are a filter! You only get the good guys, the guys that like you for YOU!" she exclaimed. With that she pulled her handbag off the counter and stormed up the stairs.

Lucky, I'm lucky? Perhaps lucky in a different way, I thought.

Soon after this, I invited Bruce to go boogie-boarding. He accepted. We had been having a lovely time together with what felt like real bonding. However, Bruce had never seen me without makeup, and there's nothing like the topsy-turvy surf pushing your board toward a sandy shoreline to remove makeup. Of course, the lead up to the occasion was filled with conversations about my angels, fear of fire, rescues, accepting outcomes.

So, the day came. The surf was sensational. The sun was bright. We laughed like crazy. And yes, my makeup wore off. We said our goodbyes and a trickle of fear told me he may not call again.

When Bruce called me the next day, I knew it was me he was smitten over. The real me, the heartfelt passionate me. I guess my roommate was right. My scars are a gift—attracting people to my heart.

• • •

Afterword

Since I began writing this book, my father died an unexpected, sudden death. Losing him shifted something deep inside of me. I savor his now forever-protected voicemail messages and the loving letters he wrote to me over the years. He didn't win any father-of-the-year awards, yet I will be eternally grateful for his pure love. As unpredictable as he was, he always appeared for his children when we needed him most. He instilled me with a passion to strive for a sense of adventure in the most mundane moments, each day. He did his best. He now lives in my heart, forever.

My husband retired from the San Diego Fire department as a Division Chief. His continuous love and devotion for my dreams makes me feel blessed.

After 56 years of living in Florida, my mother moved to Seattle for a better life. My brother Darrin, his wife Meg, and their son Luke welcomed her to be closer to them, to nourish her in her precious sunset years. As I unpacked her boxes in her new cozy bungalow, I watched her anxiety rise. I recognized her old pain of long ago when her boxes never showed up from our move from Detroit to Florida.

Yesterday's pain, if ignored, becomes today's worry and sorrow.

In my experience, events that are real gifts always come full circle. The seemingly most difficult people in our lives aren't our enemies; they are truly our greatest teachers. We must cultivate patience and appreciation for our hurt and challenges. Every one of them is an opportunity, an opportunity to love. The key is to keep our eyes and hearts open, or we may not recognize them. Or it will take more hurt and challenges to get the message.

It's been more than thirty years since I walked out of the La Costa real estate office, deflated by the broker's baseless judgment. Last week, as I pulled out of the parking space at Starbucks (just blocks from what was once his office), the same broker, one of my greatest teachers, pulled in next to me. We locked eyes as I rolled into reverse. His hair is now gray; his glasses hung on his nose.

For a moment I thought about pulling back in, and running over to share the tremendous gift his pain gave me. I wanted to thank him deeply for being unable to recognize my potential many years ago. His naiveté of my worth catapulted me into a life of bravery and healing. He truly was my greatest teacher. As I watched him get out of his car, I again briefly thought about talking with him. Suddenly, a car horn tooted behind me … asking me to move along. My signal to press forward, I thought. I drove on.

I'm eternally grateful for my experiences at UCSD and the Burn Institute. Those experiences also helped peel away the blanket of pain to reveal my worth. It was that excruciatingly disappointing time that launched my strength and courageousness to heal deeply and create Angel Faces.

It's been ten years now since the birth of Angel Faces. Our retreats are branching out to the east coast of the United States where new partners are helping us extend resources to more girls, encouraging healing to more hearts. A program for boys is next.

Piper's breast cancer is in remission, hopefully gone forever. She has embraced the many gifts cancer brings—gifts of love and appreciation for each breath we breathe. Piper can now share these gifts with Nancy, who is now enduring harsh chemotherapy treatments for her own recent diagnosis of breast cancer.

Gifts come full circle, in time. Marianne Cinat, MD, was upset and saddened when I left her cadre of the UCI burn team to start Angel Faces independently. Our relationship was strained for several years. Later, at a burn conference, I discovered that she was listed in the program as the moderator for my presentation. I was nervous.

As I walked to the stage to present, she introduced me with a crack in her voice. She shared with the room full of her peers—well respected burn/trauma surgeons—that I had worked for her, brought remarkable support programs to her burn patients then left to start my dream, my life's calling: *Angel Faces.* It was a healing moment, as though Marianne and I were the only ones in the room. Her introduction through love and respect told me that she deeply *did* support my dream. She just didn't want to lose me.

Four months later Dr. Cinat died suddenly and tragically. How fortunate I was to make peace with her before she left us. I will always hold her in the highest of light for the enormous gift of healing she shared with not only her burn and trauma patients but me.

Tiffany has now been through our level II retreat and leadership training. She volunteers with Angel Faces as a mentor for the younger girls.

Calais is now attending pre-med classes at Harvard Medical School and has goals of becoming a burn reconstructive surgeon. She and a handsome Harvard graduate are in love. So she spends what little free time she has away from studying to peek at wedding dresses. Calais is now on our Board of Directors at Angel Faces.

So I continue on my way, putting each foot forward in gratitude for my journey thus far, especially the painful events and difficult people. They truly are my greatest professors. The key is to recognize this when the next challenge comes along.

I remind myself that problems will come. It's OK to recognize them. It's okay to feel hurt. However, I must not give the problem or problematic person a "chair to sit upon" and become mired in negativity.

It takes daily reminding to trust our path even when the road sears our feet with trials and perceived problems. I am moving forward, not wasting my pain. I allow love and light to flow into me, then outward to you.

My heart feels full with the growth I reach for in myself and the people around me. With my life-long relationship with fire still transforming, I will continue to honor a fire inside my belly, sharing the warmth with those with cold hands.

Lesia Stockall Cartelli

endured a serious burn injury over 50 percent of her face and body from a natural gas explosion at the age of nine. Her grandparent's home was completely destroyed, yet her spirit survived. She transformed her pain into a life of passion and purpose. Lesia insists that we are here on Earth to do more than simply survive.

Cartelli founded Angel Faces®, a unique national nonprofit organization. Angel Faces® provides healing retreats and ongoing support that inspires adolescent girls and young women with burn/trauma injuries to achieve their optimum potential and develop meaningful relationships for them, their families, and their communities.

Resiliency and courage motivated Cartelli to face her fear of fire at age 33. She suited up in breathing apparatus, full firefighting gear, and entered a burning building known as a "control burn." Her fear conquered, she married the fire captain who led her into the fire to face her fears.

She was chosen and featured on *CNN*'s "Human Factor" with Dr. Sanjay Gupta, *HLN*, *ABC NEWS 20/20*, *Associated Press Wire* (video and print), and *PBS*, among other national TV media venues. Cartelli has received many prestigious awards for her leadership and inspiration including the Heart of a Woman Award on the *Dr. Phil Show*. She is regularly interviewed by radio stations around the world, and has been heard on Doctor Radio, Sirius and Clear Channel. *Readers Digest* and *Woman's Day* have written about her. Cartelli's own articles have been published in *USA Today*. Cartelli is a dynamic captivating internationally known motivational speaker for private corporations and medical, trauma and burn conferences.

Bring Lesia to Your Event

Lesia Stockall Cartelli is a dynamic speaker she brings both heart and humor to any event. To book Lesia for your next keynote, contact:

LesiaCartelli.com

Lesia@LesiaCartelli.com

760.846.6280